PRAYERS *for* NURSING STUDENTS

A Road to Success

NANCY WANJIRU NJOROGE

WESTBOW
PRESS®
A DIVISION OF THOMAS NELSON
& ZONDERVAN

Scripture taken from the King James Version of the Bible.

Scripture taken from the New King James Version. Copyright 1979, 1980, 1982 by Thomas Nelson, inc. Used by permission. All rights reserved.

Scripture quotations taken from the Holy Bible, New Living Translation, copyright 1996, 2004. Used by permission of Tyndale House Publishers, Inc., Wheaton, Illinois 60189. All rights reserved.

Scripture taken from the *Amplified Bible*, Copyright © 1954, 1958, 1962, 1964, 1965, 1987 by The Lockman Foundation. Used by permission.

New Revised Standard Version Bible, copyright 1989, Division of Christian Education of the National Council of the Churches of Christ in the United States of America. Used by permission. All rights reserved.

WestBow Press books may be ordered through booksellers or by contacting:

WestBow Press
A Division of Thomas Nelson & Zondervan
1663 Liberty Drive
Bloomington, IN 47403
www.westbowpress.com
1 (866) 928-1240

Because of the dynamic nature of the Internet, any web addresses or links contained in this book may have changed since publication and may no longer be valid. The views expressed in this work are solely those of the author and do not necessarily reflect the views of the publisher, and the publisher hereby disclaims any responsibility for them.

Any people depicted in stock imagery provided by Thinkstock are models, and such images are being used for illustrative purposes only.
Certain stock imagery © Thinkstock.

ISBN: 978-1-4908-9677-9 (sc)
ISBN: 978-1-4908-9676-2 (hc)
ISBN: 978-1-4908-9675-5 (e)

Library of Congress Control Number: 2015917329

Print information available on the last page.

WestBow Press rev. date: 10/06/2015

CONTENTS

DEDICATION

I want to dedicate this book to my Lord and Savior, who has helped me this far, answered my prayers, and made me become who I wanted to become. Thanks to my husband, Lenard, who was always there when I was going through this course. Thank you for your encouragement and support and for giving me hope when I almost gave up. You cooked and cleaned the house so that I could concentrate on my homework. I also want to thank my two daughters, Joy and Glorious, who never complained even when I was not able to spend much time with them because of my commitment to nursing school. Thanks to Ms. Toliver, who kept my daughters when we needed help the most. Thanks also to Pastor Basil and his wife: you played a great part with your support and prayers, which I needed every day. I cannot forget my instructors Mrs. Hardesty, Ms. Young, and Ms. Beth, who supported me throughout the course. I also thank my fellow students and friends Ms. Amber—she was always available to take me places when I could not drive myself—and my friend B., who hung out with me. We encouraged each other, did homework together, and made this happen. To everyone who touched my life during this time of difficulty, you are very much appreciated. Thank you so much, and God bless you for being there for me.

Prayers for Nursing Students

CHAPTER 1

A ROAD TO SUCCESS

Nursing as a career is very popular, and many people are changing their jobs and getting into nursing. In spite of this country's bad economy, nursing is still in demand. People are coming from other countries to the United States to do nursing. Some come and change their careers and go to nursing school.

My situation was very different. I had wanted to be a nurse since I was young. I liked the uniforms and caps, and I like helping people. In my home country, Kenya, I did not get the opportunity to go to nursing school. I did not graduate with good enough grades to go to a nursing college. A student had to have at least a grade equivalent of a C+ to be able to enroll in a teaching or nursing college. I was disappointed, but I had to change my career desire and decided to go to college to become a secretary.

After I obtained my diploma, I worked as a secretary in a secretarial bureau. My job was to type letters and manuscripts for people, and to do photocopying and word processing. After working for a year in this secretarial bureau, I got a job in another city as a school secretary. My job was to type exams and everything else that needed to be typed for the school. I worked in this school as a secretary for two years, and with my husband's help, I was able to open a secretarial-services business. For example, I typed handwritten manuscripts for people, and because home computers are not that common in Kenya, it was a very prosperous job. I had computer services, typewriters, photocopying, school curriculum textbooks, and stationery.

During this time I learned a lot from people who were writing books. Most of the manuscripts I typed for people were storybooks for children and books for high school readers. Most of the typing was challenging because the books were written in Swahili, which is harder to type than English.

I enjoyed my job, but once in a while I remembered how I wanted to become a nurse, especially because two of my friends were nurses. We went to church together, and every time we were together, I admired their jobs and their uniforms (in Kenya, nurses still wear dresses and caps). The biggest obstacle then was that there were very few opportunities for adults to go back to school in Kenya, and the few openings that existed were very expensive. I was already content with what I was doing, and I knew there was no way I could become a nurse while I was in Kenya.

After I finished high school, I wanted to go to a different country where I could better my education, but I did not have any funds. I also wanted to come to the United States, especially because the United States is associated with Canaan, but did not know how it could happen. I never wanted to do anything against God's will, but God opens ways where there are no ways. Psalm 37:5 says, "Commit your way to the Lord, trust in him, and he will act." God owns everything, and when we are struggling, he knows that we are struggling, and he will provide to us according to his riches in glory. Hagai 2:8 says, "The silver is mine and the gold is mine, declares the Lord Almighty."

"For every animal of the forest is mine and the cattle on a thousand hills. I know every bird in the mountains, and the insects in the fields are mine. If I were hungry I would not tell you, for the world is mine, and all that is in it" (Psalm 50:10–12). When someone is faithful to God, God will always be faithful. I was faithful in my job and in my church. I was committed to many activities as a wife and mother, plus pastoring a congregation of about fifty members and taking care of the poor and the sick.

One day, which was just a regular day to me, like any other day, a man brought me some papers to type and then asked me to photocopy them. This was a person I knew, and I had been seeing those kinds of papers, so I asked him what they were for. He told me to photocopy them before I filled in the details for him. "You can also photocopy them for your husband and then fill them in and send them to the United States; you might win the green card lottery," he said.

I did as he told me, and when my husband came home from work, I told him about the papers. But he had no interest in going to the United States of America.

The following day I went ahead and filled out the papers and sent them in. I forgot about them then because I was not expecting to win anything. I was content with my business because it was doing really well, but during this period the Lord started speaking to me about handing over my pastoring job. With obedience to God and a lot of struggle, and without many people understanding why I was doing it, I was able to step down as pastor, although I was still helping in the church. I also started having dreams about a very beautiful area with green grass and beautiful roads, and a lady showing me around. I did not understand what it was all about.

Three months after I sent the papers—both mine and my husband's—a letter came, saying that I had been selected among 100,000 people to go to the United States. This was unbelievable. The letter said that I should submit pictures of my whole family. It also insisted that I should not sell my property because this didn't guarantee that I would be among the lucky chosen ones. I told my husband about it, but he still was not excited about it. I pleaded with him to get pictures of the family. At the time I had only Joy and was pregnant with Glorious. We kept all this to ourselves because we did not know whether we would be able to go to the United States or not.

I sent the pictures, and then I took three days off from my business and went to a prayer center to seek God's face about this situation. Prayer centers are very common in Kenya. These are places where people go and spend time with God without doing anything else. There is no food to eat. The only thing provided is hot water. Some people carry hot chocolate or coffee, and some people decide just to drink water. There is no payment, and people stay there as long as they want. I stayed there for three days, praying and fasting, and when I came back, the power of God was upon me, but I had no confirmation whether to go to the United States or not. After about four to six months I got a letter that said I was being given one year to prepare myself to go to the United States. The letter also said to submit pictures of any changes in the family. Glorious had been added to our family, and I sent a picture of her. The letter also indicated the amount of money that was needed the day of the interview. In addition, the letter said that even after the payment and interview, there was no guarantee that we would be able to go to America. This was scary because of the amount needed and because I was afraid we might lose all our money. I kept the letter out of fear of losing the money, and forgot about it.

One day a technician who was repairing our machines came and told me to look for someone else who could repair our machines. I asked him, "Why? I have never refused to pay you." He said it was because he was going to the United States. "You have been telling me that you never wanted to go to the United States," I said. "What is going on now that you are going?"

He said, "I never wanted to go illegally, but I won a green card, so my family and I are all going." I asked him which year, and he said it was the one that ended in 2002. I told him I had won that green card, too, but that we were afraid we might lose our money. He told me go ahead and reply to the letter and look for money. "The interview is not hard if you have everything you need," he said. "God will see you through." I felt like there were bubbles coming from my heart. I was waiting for my husband to come home from work so that I could tell him this. When he came, I told him, and this time he was positive about it.

We went ahead and replied to the letter, and started selling some of our properties to raise money for the interview. It was a lot of money by then—it is still a lot to raise at one time, especially in Kenya—but God saw us through. When the day of the interview came, we had enough money. The interview went well, and we were given six months to prepare ourselves to go to the United States. There were still more hurdles to jump. We wanted money for the air tickets for four people. We had sold everything we had except our house that was under construction. We advertised it for sale, and within two months we found someone to buy the house. That gave us enough to pay for the air tickets and some left over to help us when we got there.

When this opportunity came, I remembered my desire to become a nurse and said in my heart that when I got to the United States, I would go to school to become one. When we got to the United States, life was harder than we had expected. Someone had told us that it would be easy to find a job, and others had told us that we would be given a house to live in until we could get settled. All these were nightmares. After our arrival, a friend of ours accommodated us, and we were thinking that we would find jobs within a month, but it turned out to be three months before my husband got a job. It was a very hard time for us since we had two little children and it was our first time to stay in somebody else's house. We used all the money we had—buying diapers for Glorious took a lot of it—and we felt desperate.

I felt like going back to Kenya many times, but encouragement from my husband and trusting God that things would be better helped me keep waiting. After three months we left the city of Staunton, where we were living, and went to Harrisonburg, where we were able to find a job. After two years of trying to settle down, I decided I needed to take the step of inquiring about nursing school. A friend told me about the process of applying, and I decided to apply. I passed the entrance test and was admitted, but going through the program was hard for me. It did not happen overnight. It was really a struggle, but God brought it to pass.

As you read this prayer book, you will see that it did not happen because of my own power, especially being from a different culture, but that it all happened because of God. It does not matter how long it takes when God has something for us; he will bring it to pass. I almost missed my opportunity because of fear of losing money, but God loves us so much that he will never let us miss our opportunity.

The most challenging things we faced as a family were culture shock and realizing that the high expectation of the United States having money everywhere turned out to be untrue. Although life in the United States was hard for us, especially in the beginning, I thank God that I came. Life has started to be much easier. I have touched many people's lives, which I could not have done if I were back in Kenya. I have also acquired my dream career, for which I had to wait many years. Prayer, determination, and patience have brought me to where I am today.

CHAPTER 2

WHY DO WE PRAY?

We pray so that we can have a good relationship with our Father. We also pray so that we can have fellowship with God and thank him for what he has done. We also pray to tell God our needs and our frustrations. The Bible says in the book of James 4:2, "We do not have because we do not ask." Although God knows all our needs, we still need to talk to him in prayer and tell him what we need; we have to tell him the desires of our hearts. Prayer brings changes and makes a difference in our lives.

There are many people in the Bible who touched the heart of God with their prayers. They were ordinary people like us, but after their prayers, God did extraordinary things in their lives. You can pray to and trust in God for anything, and he will bring it to pass.

In this book, I mention a few people who touched the heart of God with their prayers and God answered them. If he answered them, he can do the same for you if you trust in him. Some of those in the Bible who prayed were Hannah, Hezekiah, Elijah, Nehemiah, Jonah, Jabez, and David. I will also talk about Jesus. Jesus, being the Son of God, prayed, and we need to go deep in prayer too.

Hannah's prayers to the Lord for a son

Once when they had finished eating and drinking in Shiloh, Hannah stood up. Now Eli the priest was sitting on his chair by the doorpost of the Lord's house. In her deep anguish Hannah prayed to the Lord, weeping bitterly. And she made a vow, saying, "Lord Almighty, if you will only look on your servant's misery and remember me, and not forget your servant but give her a son, then I will give him to the Lord for all the days of his life, and no razor will ever be used on his head." As she kept on praying to the Lord, Eli observed her mouth. Hannah was praying in her heart, and her lips were moving but her voice was not heard. Eli thought she was drunk and said to her, "How long are you going to stay drunk? Put away your wine." "Not so, my lord," Hannah replied. "I am a woman who is deeply troubled. I have not been drinking wine or beer; I was pouring out my soul to the Lord. Do not take your servant for a wicked woman; I have been praying here out of my great anguish and grief." Eli answered, "Go in peace, and may the God of Israel grant you what you have asked of him." (1 Samuel 1:9–17)

Sometimes it is hard to understand God, but we need to trust in him, whatever comes our way. Hannah was a faithful woman, but she had no children. Her womb was shut for some unknown reason. She was depressed because during her time, a woman without children was looked down upon, but she knew the Lord her God. It is very important to know our God and to understand that in difficult situations, he will be with us. Sometimes we do not understand why we go through hard times, but God is going to answer us when we turn to him in prayer.

When I went through nursing school, I prayed like Hannah because I needed education. I wanted to become a nurse, but I knew it could not happen unless I turned to God in prayer. Sometimes I cried bitterly like Hannah, thinking that maybe I would not make it through, but finally, with prayer, God saw me through.

Eli the priest could not understand Hannah when she was praying to God because he could not hear her even though her lips were moving. Sometimes people will not understand us, but in every situation, turn to God in prayer. Hannah explained to Eli how troubled she was, and explained that she was not drunk. Sometimes in life we are troubled, in our studies especially because we have so many responsibilities. When we think of cooking, cleaning the house, doing homework, and going to work, we can get to the point of breaking down, and we need prayer to support us so that we can keep receiving strength to help us keep moving. The Bible says that the Lord will renew the strength of those who wait upon him. God is going to renew your strength as you keep waiting for him. After Hannah's prayer, God granted Hannah her request.

I do not know what you are praying for; maybe you have failed your National Council Licensure Examination(NCLEX) many times. I am here to tell you that you can do it. Pray like Hannah, and God will grant your request. Pick up your books, look for professional tutors, put God first in prayers, and you will succeed. I have gone through it, and I have come out successfully.

National Council Licensure Examination (NCLEX) is an exam that is required by the board of nursing in United States. It is a requirement for every nurse after finishing the program to test for this exam and pass in order to practice. It can be discouraging for a nurse to go through the program and not pass NCLEX because he / she cannot practice as a nurse no matter how skilled he / she is.

Hezekiah prayed when he learned that he was going to die.

In those days Hezekiah became ill and was at the point of death. The prophet Isaiah son of Amoz went to him and said, "This is what the Lord says: Put your house in order, because you are going to die; you will not recover." Hezekiah turned his face to the wall and prayed to the Lord, "Remember, Lord, how I have walked before you faithfully and with wholehearted devotion and have done what is good in your eyes." And Hezekiah wept bitterly. Before Isaiah had left the middle court, the word of the Lord came to him: "Go back and tell Hezekiah, the ruler of my people, 'This is what the Lord, the God of your father David, says: I have heard your prayer and seen your tears; I will heal you. On the third day from now you will go up to the temple of the Lord. I will add fifteen years to your life. And I will deliver you and this city from the hand of the king of Assyria. I will defend this city for my sake and for the sake of my servant David.'" Then Isaiah said, "Prepare a poultice of figs." They did so and applied it to the boil, and he recovered.

Hezekiah had asked Isaiah, "What will be the sign that the Lord will heal me and that I will go up to the temple of the Lord on the third day from now?" Isaiah answered, "This is the Lord's sign to you that the Lord will do what he has promised: Shall the shadow go forward ten steps, or shall it go back ten steps?" "It is a simple matter for the shadow to go forward ten steps," said Hezekiah. "Rather, have it go back ten steps." Then the prophet Isaiah called on the Lord, and the Lord made the shadow go back the ten steps it had gone down on the stairway of Ahaz. (2 Kings 20:1–11)

The prayer and cry of Hezekiah resembles the cry of Hannah. Hannah prayed and cried bitterly to the Lord, Hezekiah prayed and cried bitterly to the Lord, and God saw his tears. How many times have you cried before the Lord? He is going to see your tears. Can God change his mind when we pray? Yes, he can. Hezekiah was sick and Isaiah the prophet was sent to him to tell him to keep his house in order because he was going to die. Hezekiah was not ready to die, and he cried to the Lord his God. Does prayer change things? Yes, prayer changes hard situations if we trust in God.

Hezekiah reminded God of the things he had done for him, and he also cried bitterly. Is there anything that you have done for the Lord that you can remind him about when things are hard, you're in an unfavorable situation, and you are not doing well on your exams or tests or in your homework? Look back at your life and see the things you have done for the Lord. The Bible says before Isaiah the prophet left the court, the Lord spoke to him and told him to go back and tell Hezekiah that the Lord had heard his prayers and seen his tears. How many times have you cried because things in your life were so hard? As student nurses, we find that many things make us cry. God has seen your tears and is going to help you out. Maybe you are frustrated because of clinical, and dosage calculations, which are very common in most nursing schools. God has heard your prayers and has seen your tears. Keep holding on. If God can add fifteen years for Hezekiah, he is the same God who can help you out in nursing school. Hezekiah wanted to know for sure that the Lord had spoken and asked Isaiah for a sign, which was granted to him. The shadow went backward instead of forward ten times; this shows that nothing is impossible with God. He can give us whatever we ask for. He controls nature; the Bible says the earth and the fullness thereof belong to him.

As students we have many needs. Some of us are unable to work full-time because of the demands of our schoolwork. Others of us have children and are single mothers and single dads, but God knows all our needs, and he will meet them according to his riches in glory. He knew that you would become a nurse before the foundation of the earth, he knows that you like helping others, and he is going to grant your request just as he did Hezekiah's.

I was brought up in a rural area of Kenya. During this time many people did not have watches or radios. We depended on birds singing in the morning to wake us up to get ready for school. Maybe this sounds weird to you, but it reminds me about appreciating God's creation. We also depended on shadow so that we could tell what time it was. Thank God Kenya is a tropical country with only two seasons: rainy and sunny, which meant there was no snow to cover the shadow. The shadow always goes forward, but when the sun is setting, it looks like it is on the side. Still it doesn't move backward; it still goes forward. For Hezekiah to know it was really God who was giving him a promise of life, he asked if the shadow could go backward, and it happened without changing the time of the day. If God can take a shadow backward, he is the same God who can help you in your studies. Trust him in big things, and he will bring them to pass.

The problem we have in this generation is giving up so easily. After failing once or twice, we just call it quits. I am encouraging you to keep trying and not give up. You are not what people say you are but who God says you are. I almost believed who I was not because of being labeled by people who did not know who I was. Only God has your final word, and he is going to see you through.

Elijah prayed for the rain and it did not rain for three and a half years.

Elijah Announces a Great Drought

Now Elijah the Tishbite, from Tishbe in Gilead, said to Ahab, "As the Lord, the God of Israel, lives, whom I serve, there will be neither dew nor rain in the next few years except at my word." (1 Kings 17:1)

Elijah was a human being like us, but he prayed an extraordinary prayer and told King Ahab with confidence that it would not rain, or even dew, for the next few years. What confidence in God. Our God controls the rain, sun, snow, everything, and he can control your studies and exams. The Lord wants us to trust him and pray with confidence. As nurses we are trained to take care of others. We need to have confidence in God because we have others looking unto us and cannot manage lives without his help. Elijah knew his God; he not only knew him but believed and trusted in him. In our studies we need to trust him and believe we cannot do it by our own power. We need the confidence of Elijah and to face each challenge of life with confidence. Confession is the key to success. Start confessing that you can do it.

When I was going through the licensed practical nursing program, I was always confessing, "I can do all things through Christ who strengthens me." You need to start confessing even when it looks dark because before dawn there is the darkest hour. Your dawn is coming. Do not listen to the lies of the enemy but focus on the Word of God. Our words hold a miracle. Life and death are in the power of the tongue. Elijah told King Ahab, "It will not rain except at my word." So when Elijah kept quiet about the issue of rain, it did not rain. Can you imagine the kind of disaster everyone faced because of the disobedience of King Ahab? Everybody in Israel at this time suffered, but Elijah was taken care of by ravens.

I remember when I was young, there was famine in Kenya on two different occasions. Kenya depends on its own agriculture for about 75% of its food, and normally there is no preservation of food apart from drying the grains and putting some powder pesticide on it to prevent it from being infested by weevils. During this period there was no rain for about two years, and it was hard for people to get anything to eat. I remember my older brother going to the city to line up for corn flour. Sometimes he would spend hours in line, but by the time it was his turn, the flour was already gone. It was discouraging for him and for the whole family. It does not matter who or what causes the drought, it affects everyone in the area, even the animals. Ahab's disobedience had caused everyone, even the innocent, to suffer during this period of time, but Elijah had food to eat and water to drink from a brook. Even when things do not look promising, God is going to take care of his people. When you keep God first and continue trusting in him, he is going to meet your need.

Sometimes in my studies it looked like there was no hope. I doubted my capabilities, I cried many times, and I felt sad when some of my classmates quit because of low grades. I knew it was only because of God's great mercy that I got through it. Whatever you are going through, you can make it if you pray and trust in God. Look unto Jesus because that is where your help comes from. David, in Psalm 121: 1-2 says, I lift up my eyes to the mountains-where does my help come from? My help comes from the Lord, the marker of heaven and earth. Your help does not come from the mountains; it comes from the Creator of the universe, so keep trusting in him. Because of Elijah's faith, he is also mentioned in James 5:17. Shutting the heavens looks more complicated than passing NCLEX or going through nursing school, but both require faith and prayers. If Elijah was just ordinary like us and he did shut the heavens and there was no rain for three and a half years, you can also pray and bring your dream to pass.

We Can Conquer the Giant

> David said to the Philistine, "You come against me with sword and spear and javelin, but I come against you in the name of the Lord Almighty, the God of the armies of Israel, whom you have defied.

This day the Lord will deliver you into my hands, and I'll strike you down and cut off your head. This very day I will give the carcasses of the Philistine army to the birds and the wild animals, and the whole world will know that there is a God in Israel. All those gathered here will know that it is not by sword or spear that the Lord saves; for the battle is the Lord's, and he will give all of you into our hands." (1 Samuel 17:45–47)

There is power in the words we speak. The story of David and Goliath is a very powerful story that helps us understand that we do not conquer because of our body size but because of the power that God has given us and the confessions of our mouths. Goliath spoke to David, trying to mock him or intimidate him. David also spoke to Goliath, telling him that he was going to defeat him in the name of the Lord almighty. There is a giant ahead of you, trying to intimidate you and show you that you cannot make it in life. There is that huge final exam that worries you because if you do not pass it, you will be kicked out of the program. Do not pay attention to that giant just as David did not pay attention to Goliath's words; he knew that greater was he who was in him than the one who was in Goliath. Do not allow the negative thoughts to rule your mind and tell you that you cannot make it.

I believe those people who saw David's size were wondering, *What is he thinking? Does he not see the size of Goliath?* But David knew that the Lord who was in him was bigger than Goliath. You have a seed of success and power and greatness in your life. Do not allow the enemy to steal it from you. Your giant will try to speak back to you by trying to remove the seed you already have. Negative thoughts will try to get into your mind, telling you it is not going to happen. Do not listen to those negative thoughts but continue confessing the Word of God. Speak of how big your God is.

There is power in spoken words. The Bible says in Proverbs 18:21 that "death and life are in the power of the tongue and they who love it shall eat the fruit thereof". What are you saying about your situation? You have the power to turn your situation around. Maybe you have failed your NCLEX many times and have already given up. I have good news for you: do not give up even if the NCLEX looks like a huge giant. Speak God's Word, pray, and trust in him, and he will see you through.

David's brothers were not nice to him. They tried to tell him to go back to take care of the sheep; they even told him, "You are just here so that you can watch the battle." But David was there for a reason and a purpose. Maybe people have told you that nursing is not your career, or that you will never pass the NCLEX. Do not go with what people say but with what the Word of God says about your life. I want to let you know that it was God's divine purpose for you to go to school, and he will not bring you this far and leave you alone. There is always another chance, and God has another chance for you. Encourage yourself and stand up again and start over. It is not too late. Maybe you are already depressed because you have tried to do your NCLEX several times. Do not lose hope; just try one more time because with God, all things are possible.

When I was young and in children's Sunday school, we used to say this before we could start class: "My God is so big, so strong, and so mighty that there is nothing my God cannot do." Your God is bigger than your exams, tests, or NCLEX. The Bible says, "Try me, and I will open the windows of heaven." Take a step and try God, speak to him and tell him what you have been going through, ask people to pray with you, look for professionals to help you study, and as David defeated Goliath, in the same way you will be able to pass your exams or NCLEX.

Prayer of Nehemiah

Building the Wall of Jerusalem

> When I heard these things, I sat down and wept. For some days I mourned and fasted and prayed before the God of heaven. Then I said: "Lord, the God of heaven, the great and awesome God, who keeps his covenant of love with those who love him and keep his commandments, let your ear be attentive and your eyes open to hear the prayer your servant is praying before you day and night for your servants, the people of Israel. I confess the sins we Israelites, including myself and my father's family, have committed against you. We have acted very wickedly toward you. We have not obeyed the commands, decrees and laws you gave your servant Moses. Remember the instruction you gave your servant Moses, saying, 'If you are unfaithful, I will scatter you among the nations, but if you return to me and obey my commands, then even if your exiled people are at the farthest horizon, I will gather them from there and bring them to the place I have chosen as a dwelling for

my Name.' They are your servants and your people, whom you redeemed by your great strength and your mighty hand. Lord, let your ear be attentive to the prayer of this your servant and to the prayer of your servants who delight in revering your name. Give your servant success today by granting him favor in the presence of this man." I was cupbearer to the king. (Nehemiah 1:4–11)

In Kenya, building a wall before building the house is very important. When I first came to the United States, I was surprised to see that houses are not surrounded by walls. In Kenya, it is important to have a fence around a house for safety and protection. Most people build a wall and put broken bottles on top to prevent burglars from getting into the house. Those who are able also hire a gatekeeper day and night to prevent enemies or thugs from getting in. The thugs who are determined still climb on top of the fence and get inside and break into the house. Occasionally, the fence costs even more than building the house because people make walls very strong. Building the wall was important to Nehemiah at this time because of safety. Building the wall also symbolized peace and strength. That is why he had the burden to build the wall of Jerusalem.

It does not matter who you are: you can make a difference in a nation and in other people's lives. Nehemiah was just a cupbearer to the king, but he had a heart for other people. When he heard about the wall of Jerusalem being broken, he was touched. He prayed and fasted, and he reminded God what he had said about his children: that if they are unfaithful, God will scatter them among the nations, but if they return to him and obey his commands, he will gather them and bring them to the place he has chosen as a dwelling for his name. This was a strong prayer and a huge commitment. Nehemiah prayed for success and asked God to grant him favor before the king. Nehemiah did not just pray and cry; he also fasted.

There are times we need to not only pray and cry before God but deny ourselves and fast. Jesus fasted, too, which was when the Devil tried to tempt him to change stones into bread. For us to receive success in our studies, we need to pray and sometimes also to fast. We also need to carry other people's burden. If you see your fellow students struggling, encourage them and lift them up in prayers. You can also go ahead and fast on their behalf. Nehemiah fasted on behalf of the Jews. In the same way, you can fast on behalf of your fellow students. The Bible says for us to carry other people's burdens and also to pray for one another. I have prayed and fasted for other people—you do not have to tell them that you are praying for them—and I have seen God answer prayers. Nehemiah received favor from the king, and was granted permission to go and build the wall of Jerusalem.

Do you need favor to pass your exam? Pray and fast and seek God's will for your life. The Bible says in Mathew 6:33, "Seek ye first the kingdom of God and his righteousness and other things shall be added unto you." Be faithful in prayers and God's Word, and other things, including your exams, NCLEX, and tests will be added unto you. Although Nehemiah received favor, it was not that easy to build the wall of Jerusalem. There were obstacles, but he did not give up. You might face opposition when you are trying to accomplish your dreams, but this does not mean that you do not have the favor of God. Tobiah tried to discourage Nehemiah, saying even a fox can jump on this fence.

It doesn't matter what you are doing; you will find critics, people who talk against you, and people who think you cannot make it. If you are trying to start over and study or go to school again, critics will say, "She just failed her exam, and now she is trying to go back to school again." Do not listen to critics. Keep doing what God has called you to do. You will face Tobiahs and Sanballats on your way who will discourage you and even make you think you are not doing the right thing or that you are not capable, but do not give up. "Keep building your wall" and God will see you through. When Sanballat heard that the wall of Jerusalem was built, he was angry and greatly enraged, and he mocked the Jews. Do not be surprised when your enemies get angry after you pass your exams or NCLEX and start to mock you. Keep praising God for your success and learn to praise God for others' success too.

The Prayer of Jonah

From inside the fish Jonah prayed to the Lord his God. He said: "In my distress I called to the Lord, and he answered me. From deep in the realm of the dead I called for help, and you listened to my cry. You hurled me into the depths, into the very heart of the seas, and the currents swirled about me; all your waves and breakers swept over me. I said, 'I have been banished from your sight; yet I will look again toward your holy temple.' The engulfing waters threatened me, the deep surrounded me; seaweed was wrapped around my head. To the roots of the mountains I sank down; the earth beneath barred me in forever. But you, Lord my God, brought my life up from the pit. When my life was ebbing away, I remembered you, Lord, and my prayer rose to you, to your holy temple. Those who cling to worthless idols turn away from God's love for them. But I, with shouts of grateful praise, will sacrifice to you. What I have vowed I will make good. I will say, 'Salvation comes from the Lord.'" And the Lord commanded the fish, and it vomited Jonah onto dry land. (Jonah 2:1–10)

The story of Jonah is amazing. God called him and sent him to Nineveh to go talk to the people and tell them to repent. Nineveh was to be destroyed, but Jonah knew that the Lord was merciful and would not destroy them, so he refused to go to Nineveh and started a journey to Tarshish. There was a strong wave, and Jonah was sleeping. He was thrown into the sea, where the fish swallowed him. He was in the belly of the fish for three days and three nights. While in the belly, he prayed for God's mercy, and miraculously, the fish vomited him and he landed at Nineveh. If Jonah prayed while in the fish's belly, you can pray no matter what you are going through and no matter where you are. I believe it was very uncomfortable for Jonah in the fish's belly, but that is where he cried unto the Lord his God, and God answered his prayers. He went to Nineveh and preached the gospel, and Nineveh was not destroyed.

It doesn't matter where we are; God will answer our prayers. Sometimes we become so disobedient that we want to do what we want to do. We do not want to listen to God's command. We want to go to areas that will suit us—areas that are comfortable and where we do not have to pay a price. That is exactly what Jonah was doing. In our studies we have to pay the price. It is not easy to go through college, whether you are studying nursing or not. Where does the Lord want you to go? Are you heading to Nineveh or are you going to Tarshish?

In life sometimes we feel like we are in the belly of the fish. I believe it was uncomfortable for Jonah inside the fish, but he remembered to pray. Most of the time while I was in school, I was stressed, nervous, and worried about making it, but I believe Jonah was worse in the fish's belly than I was. When we are in hard situations, the only one who can deliver us is God. When your studies seem hard, do not give up; keep praying, and the Lord will see you through.

Let us listen to God's voice so that we can know his direction. After prayer and listening to him, he will guide us and help us pick the right answers on the exam. I have seen people throwing up before exams. One student told me that she cried all through her NCLEX because she was afraid of failing. I do not know how she passed it because if I start crying, I cannot think right. Do not be rebellious like Jonah but trust in the Lord and know that whoever started a good work in you will come to accomplish it. Whoever directed you to go to school knew how busy you are, he knew your capabilities, he knew you could become a good nurse, and he will see you through.

The Prayer of Jabez

"Jabez cried out to the God of Israel, 'Oh, that you would bless me and enlarge my territory! Let your hand be with me, and keep me from harm so that I will be free from pain.' And God granted his request" (1 Chronicles 4:10).

God granted Jabez his request, and he is the same God who can grant us our request when we ask him in faith. When we cry to him about our studies, he will see us through. I can testify to that because he has seen me through. Those who come from other countries and go to school here know how hard it is for us to fit into American culture and into the school curriculum, but as he did to Jabez, he has been doing to us. Jabez was more honored than his brothers. His mother gave birth to him in pain. Jabez means "born in pain" or "pain." Jabez cried out to the Lord of Israel, saying, "Oh, that you would bless me and enlarge my territory!" Jabez knew that his life would be filled with pain if he did not turn around and ask for God's blessing. Although he was more honored than his brothers, there was no way this honor could have come to pass without Jabez praying the prayers of blessing.

You need to pray prayers of blessings over your life and over your family, children, and friends. Jabez's mother spoke of pain when he was born. The words of our parents are very strong, but we need to know that we can stand on God's promises and turn every negative word spoken to us around. It doesn't matter who has spoken those negative words; maybe it is your teacher when you were growing up, maybe it was your parents or your boss. You have power and authority to change those words and walk in God's promises. Jabez asked God to free him from pain. I believe this was not physical pain but emotional pain. You might be going through emotional pain because of something that has happened in your life or because somebody has done something to you. Ask God to set you free from pain.

Some people think that Jabez was selfish, asking God to bless him, but I believe there is a time that we have to stand for ourselves and no one else can stand for us. We need to stand up and break every curse in our life. It may be something our parents did. Maybe they did it in ignorance, not thinking it would affect their children. What did your mother or your father say about you? What name were you given when you were born? Do you need to speak blessing upon your own life? God granted Jabez his request. God is going to grant you your request if you call on and trust in him. The Lord is ready to enlarge your territory. It is not the end of your blessings. The wonders are yet to come.

Jabez asked God to keep him from harm so that he would be free from pain. Can you imagine how Jabez's life was before he started praying these prayers? I believe he went through difficulties until he came to the point of knowing about his life and the meaning of his name. Both of my children were born out of very severe pain. I cannot remember any other time in my life when I have experienced the pain that I experienced during the birth of my two girls. I don't think epidurals were available in Kenya then, and if they were, no one offered one to me, and I bore them naturally. The pain was so severe that I lost consciousness, but even after going through all that pain, I did not name them anything related to the pain.

My firstborn is Joy. She brought a lot of joy to our family when she was born, and she still does. She has been very responsible with her own things and also about taking care of her little sister. The second one is Glorious. I see God's glory in her life. She is so caring that she never wants to upset anybody, and when she does, she wants to reconcile as quickly as she can. She is a pleasure to be around.

Young mothers, be careful about the names you give to your children. God honored Jabez's prayer. God will honor your prayers; have faith in God. As you read the story of Jabez, I want you to understand that you can pray for anything. Jabez's prayers are very different from other people's prayers in the Bible. Maybe you have never thought of praying for your studies. You just take it for granted and say you are a C student, and that is what you get. You need to change your mentality and start asking God for an A. Jabez asked God for blessing—and not only one blessing; he said that you may bless me indeed. This shows he asked for abundant blessing.

Sometimes we ask too little, thinking that we are not supposed to have much. Whenever I am taking a class, I ask God for an A. I used to ask him for a C, but I have known better than C, so now I ask for the best. I know that he can give abundantly, exceedingly, beyond what I can even ask for. I am always asking for more. Ask God to bless your studies indeed. Ask him to extend your territory. You do not want just to be a certified aide; ask him for what you want. Do you want to be a registered nurse? Tell him and he will extend your territory. Do you want to become a nurse practitioner? It is not too late; you can still do it. Psalm 2:8 says ask for a nation and he will give it unto you. This means you can ask for anything by prayer and he will grant your request. It is not too late to ask for success in your studies.

Prayer of Jesus Before Crucifixion

> Then He said to them, "My soul is exceedingly sorrowful, even to death. Stay here and watch with Me." He went a little farther and fell on His face,

and prayed, saying, "O My Father, if it is possible, let this cup pass from Me; nevertheless, not as I will, but as You will." Then He came to the disciples and found them sleeping, and said to Peter, "What! Could you not watch with Me one hour? Watch and pray, lest you enter into temptation. The spirit indeed is willing, but the flesh is weak." Again, a second time, He went away and prayed, saying, "O My Father, if this cup cannot pass away from me unless I drink it, your will be done." (Matthew 26:38–42 NKJV)

Have you ever thought of something bad happening in your life, or has something bad happened in your life that you were unable to prevent? I had a car accident last year. I knew it was going to happen, but I did not know how to prevent it. I was taking my girls to school, and it had snowed the previous day. I am not sure, but I think I hit black ice. My car felt like it was moving in the air. I thought of hitting the brakes, but I heard a voice telling me, "Do not hit the brakes." I am glad I obeyed the Holy Spirit because hitting the brakes might have wrecked my car more than it was wrecked. Just after the bridge, my car hit the guardrail, turned 360 degrees, and was completely wrecked in front. The bumper came out. I was not able to drive it again right away. Before this happened, I was reading Psalm 91 about God's protection. I was able to thank God for his protection and quote the promises in Psalm 91.

Sometimes when you know for sure that a loved one will die, it is normal to be scared and stressed. We try to hope for the best, we deny everything, and we tell ourselves that it is going to be all right. Jesus knew very well that he was going to die. It was a very painful last moment for him. He prayed to his father to remove the cup from him. He knew it was going to be a painful death. He asked his father for his will to be done. There is a time in life we just need to ask God for his will to be done. Some things that happen in life are not very easy, but we just need to surrender to God and ask for his will to be done.

There are also times we need to separate ourselves from our loved ones and go someplace at a distance to seek the face of the Lord. We need to move away from our comfort zone and seek God's face. Sometimes we do not hear God when we are in our comfort zone. We need to deny our life and move out so that we can hear God speaking. The Bible says in Psalm 46:10, "Be still and know that I am God, I am exalted among the Nations, I am exalted among the earth." It is hard to be still when we are surrounded by different things and everyday activities. When I was in Kenya, I was pastoring a congregation of about fifty people. In Kenya, we have prayer centers as well as mountains where people go and pray, and it was safe at that time. Every three months I was separating myself from my family for a week and sometimes three days to go to a prayer center to pray for the church and to know God's guidance for his people. After these prayers I always had a message for the church and felt stronger than before. I would come back and hold open-air meetings (preaching outside), and the meetings were very successful. I am looking forward to doing this again in the future.

We all need a close relationship with God where we can pour out our spirit to him without disturbances. If Jesus had to separate himself from his disciples, we also need to separate ourselves from our jobs, friends, and day-to-day activities. The same thing is true with our education: when things get hard, we need to separate ourselves and have time with God. The separation does not mean you pack your things and go somewhere. You can separate yourself by creating time to pray for your success in education. Set a time to talk to God and ask him his will for your life. Sometimes the studies get so hard that we get to the point of asking ourselves, *Does God really want me to do this?* You are not the first one to ask God a question. Jesus got to the point that it was so hard for him, he asked his father to remove the cup from him—if it was his will. What is God's will for our studies, especially for us nurses, who are looking forward to helping others? It is God's will for us to excel in our education.

"If you listen to these commands of the Lord your God that I am giving you today, and if you carefully obey them, the Lord will make you the head and not the tail, and you will always be on top and never at the bottom" (Deuteronomy 28:13 NLT). Most of the times when going through school you need to separate yourself from everything that will prevent you from achieving your dream. There are things we cannot accomplish in life if we are still hanging around with others who do not have the same call we do. Jesus separated himself from his disciples. He took the closest disciples with him, but still they could not stay awake when Jesus was praying. They did not understand the weight that Jesus had on his shoulders. Sometimes it is only the person who is going through something that knows the weight.

Nursing school has a lot of demands and requires homework, taking tests, and writing papers. If we keep hanging around with people who are not called as we are, it is hard to accomplish our goal. This does not mean that you leave your friends and family. It means that you let your family know what you are doing so that they can be supportive of you. Inform them that sometimes you will not be available for them because of the demands of your schoolwork. Ask your friends and family members if they can help you clean your house or babysit your children while you are doing your homework. Let them understand that at some point you will be free to socialize and even to attend gatherings but that right now the most important thing is to study and to commit your studies in the Lord. If Jesus was the Son of God and he prayed, we also need to spend time with God in prayers to succeed in life.

CHAPTER 3

THERE IS NOTHING TOO HARD FOR THE LORD

T his book is written to inspire student nurses and to let them know that prayers, hard work, determination, and a good attitude will help them accomplish their dreams. As the journey starts, you will see that student nurses succeed because of prayers. You can join in prayers, especially if you are in nursing school; you cannot make it without God's help. Enjoy this journey to success, and God will richly bless you.

"Call to me and I will answer you and tell you great and unsearchable things you do not know" (Jeremiah 33:3). When we call unto the Lord, he will answer us and reveal great things, dreams, and gifts we do not even know about. I love writing, especially Christian materials, but I never thought I could get to the point of writing something that would be published and help others. There are things in your heart that you may not know about, but when you call unto the Lord, he will be ready to reveal them to you.

"I am the Lord, the God of all mankind. Is anything too hard for me?" (Jeremiah 32:27). This book consists of prayers that I prayed when I was taking classes in nursing school to become a licensed practical nurse (LPN). It was a hard journey for me, especially being a foreigner with English as my second language. Being new to the United States made it even harder for me during this time. Sometimes I doubted myself, and I worried myself to death. I got to the point of thinking I was someone I was not, but God saw me through in all my weakness. I had to trust in him and understand his Word that there is nothing too hard for him. The Bible says in Joel 3:10 Let the weakling say, "I am strong!" With this experience I have grown more in spirit, and I know I can do all things through Christ who strengthens me, according to Philippians 4:13. I have become a positive person more than ever before.

Whatever you may be going through, do not doubt your potential. If I got through nursing school, especially coming from a different culture, you can do it also. It is because of prayer and dedicated instructors that I am where I am today. I was treated differently, especially because I am quiet by nature and from a different culture, and many people thought I would not make it. I became fearful, and sometimes I was angry because of the way people were treating me. I had no one to relate with. I tried to befriend people, but for some unknown reason, no one wanted to befriend me, and because of this, my journey became much harder. I also felt like I was singled out and stereotyped. I started searching my heart, which made me go deeper into searching God's face.

No one else has the final word for you except God. There is a song sung in Kenya that goes, "Who has the final say?" Jesus has the final say. He will always bring your dream to pass. During this difficult situation God was always there for me. I could not have made it without prayers; it was a challenging time in my life. I thought of quitting many times, but I could hear a small voice in my heart telling me, "It is not time to give up." My loving husband, Lenard, also encouraged me, and God gave me hope throughout the course. I had written this Scripture many places in my house: "I can do all things through Christ who strengthens me" (Philippians 4:13). I made it through because of prayers and self-confidence. "It was not by might nor by power but by the Holy Spirit, says the Lord" (Zachariah 4:6). You can pray these prayers in your day-to-day life. You do not have to be a nurse to pray. You can be having a difficult time in your life with your career, your health, or your family. Or maybe you have other things going on. This book can change your life or the life of a loved one. These are real-life prayers.

CHAPTER 4

COMMITTING STUDIES
TO THE LORD

September 5, 2006

I n May 2006 I had to commit my studies to the Lord as I was going through school to become a licensed practical nurse.

"Commit to the Lord whatever you do, and He will establish your plans" (Proverbs 16:3). Lord, I need you in my studies. I cannot make it without you. Sometimes I am so nervous, I need your help. Other times I have negative thoughts; please help me fight them. Give me confidence within myself, and help me learn and understand new terminology. I know I can make it, for many have passed through this journey and come out successfully. When terminology is so hard to pronounce and remember, please help me. Help me go through the challenges with confidence. Even when schoolwork is too much, help me to love my family all the more and to continue taking care of them.

You helped me with dosage calculations. I got an A just because of your help. I am waiting upon you to help me in pharmacology. Help me to understand the nursing process, think critically, and perform everything my instructors want me to do. I rely on you in everything and thank you for being present every moment. I need you. In Jesus' name, amen.

In order to succeed, you must have a positive attitude and faith in God. My God is so big, so strong, and so mighty that there is nothing he cannot do. "But seek first his kingdom and his righteousness and all these things will be given to you as well" (Matthew 6:33).

September 6, 2006

L ord, I pray for knowledge that comes from you. Just as you gave wisdom to Solomon, I pray that you will give me wisdom in this nursing career. Help me not to fear. Help me not to see others as better or more special than me. I know you have made me extra special and that with your help I can make it. Let your grace be sufficient for me even at this time. For the quiz and test tomorrow and Friday, I need your help. Help me also to understand the words and the accent clearly. Let your favor and the favor from the instructors be upon me.

Psalm 39:14 says I am fearful and wonderfully made. I am made in God's image. When God looks at me, he does not see a failure; he sees a victor, a conqueror, a warrior. In Jesus' name, amen. "For you created my inmost being; you knit me together in my mother's womb. I praise you because I am fearfully and wonderfully made; your works are wonderful, I know that full well" (Psalm 139:13–14).

CHAPTER 5

"THIS FAR THE LORD HAS HELPED ME"

September 7, 2006

L ord, I want to thank you for bringing me this far. You are my Ebenezer. "This far you have brought me." I am so scared and asking myself so many questions. Please help me. I have a lot of work ahead of me. As I keep going to class, I keep asking myself whether I'll make it. The instructors are telling us not to have stinking thinking. Please, Lord, help me, and do not let me down. Sometimes I do not understand. I do not even know how other students feel, but I pray for them also. I have a test tomorrow, and I am so scared. Let your grace be sufficient for me. Help me this night that I may understand what I am going to study so that I can get a 78, which is the passing score tomorrow. In Jesus' name I pray. "Pray and it will be granted unto you."

I know it is just because of God's love and mercy that I am where I am. I continue to call him Ebenezer, "this far he has helped me." He has enabled me to face each day, one at a time. I know the one who has brought me this far will help me until the end. "Then

Samuel took a stone and set it up between Mizpah and Shen. He named it Ebenezer, saying, 'This far the Lord has helped us'" (1 Samuel 7:12).

September 8, 2006

Lord, I thank you for answering my prayers. I prayed for a C and you gave me a B. Thank you for giving me more than I asked for. That is what your Word says: "Give and it will be given to you. A good measure, pressed down, shaken together and running over, will be poured into your lap. For with the measure you use, it will be measured to you" (Luke 6:38). You always fulfill the desires of my heart. Thank you for giving me good kids and understanding instructors. I pray for Miss Y., for the desire she has for all the students to pass. Give her enough strength to be able to teach. Let her not have any sorrow when teaching or when things become too much for her. As she imparts knowledge to the students, impart wisdom in her so that she will know how to handle each and every student. As I study this weekend, help me to follow Mrs. H.'s instructions. Help me to finish her paper in time. In Jesus' name I pray, amen.

September 12, 2006

Lord, sometimes it is too hard for me. I do not know where to start, especially when I am going to work. Yesterday I thought it was too much, but after getting to class today, they added an article to be ready on Friday. I am still worried. I do not know how to handle myself, my family, and my job; I need your help, God. Without you I cannot make it. I do not know whether it is going to be easy anymore. It sounds like it is going to be more and more. The test on Thursday scares me a lot, followed by a test on Friday. Help me, Lord, that I get 78 percent, which is the passing mark. As I study tonight, give me enough grace and understanding as I pray, believing and trusting in Jesus' name. Amen.

September 13, 2006

Lord, I thank you for this day. You have been so good to me. Help me, oh Lord, in this program. Help me as I study tonight for the test. You are so loving, and I cannot do it without you. I do not know how the test will be. Direct me in the right paths. Help me to study and understand. I am trusting in you that you will help me get 78 percent. When I do not know how to plan my days and hours, I need you to help me.

Mrs. H. said there will be more and more work when we start clinical. Help me not to fall behind. Help me to turn in my work on time. I do not want to be a student who makes things hard on instructors. Help me also to take it one day at a time without fear. I am not very organized right now, and I want you to help me in this area. Please help me in my weaknesses. Help also the other students who are feeling the way I am feeling. With your help, I know I'll make it. In Jesus' name, amen.

September 14, 2006

Lord, I thank you. You are a miracle-working God. I can't believe what I got; you surprised me. Thank you for your surprise. I just give you all the praise and all the honor. You are so wonderful. You are a marvelous God. Thanks for helping me pass that skin cancer and burn test. It was wonderful getting an A. You always give beyond what I expected. I also pray for Mrs. H., for giving us that kind of a test. I didn't know that she would test us on exactly what we learned. May God bless her for that.

Tomorrow I have another test. I need your help, oh Lord. I can't make it without you. Help me as I study. Sometimes it is so hard when I have my husband and children, but with you, I'll make it. Help also my husband to succeed in his studies. In Jesus' name I pray, amen. "Every good and perfect gift is from above, coming down from the Father of the heavenly lights, who does not change like shifting shadows" (James 1:17).

September 25, 2006

Lord, I thank you for all these days you have been on my side. The schoolwork is too much for me. Ms. Y. said I need to take it one day at a time. Lord, help me to do exactly that. Lord, we have a lot of assignments, and Mrs. H. gives us quizzes every day. I do not know if I'll make it, but I need your help. I cannot do it without you. I am also stressed because of work. Most of the time I am having very hard days at work. Please, I need your help. Other students might be having the same problems, and I pray for them too. Help me to adjust where necessary. I also need your help to study and pass the three tests I'll take on Tuesday. I am also not familiar with Assessment Technology Institute(ATI). I need your help. In Jesus' name I pray, amen.

ATI- offers review programs designed to increase students pass rates on the nursing licensing exam. It also increases confidence and familiarity with exam content. ATI provides books, on line practice questions and proctored testing over the major content areas in nursing. During this time the instructors started introducing the students to ATI questions so that they can be familiar with the type of questions that are brought by National Council Licensure Examination (NCLEX).

September 28, 2006

Lord, I am so excited. I give you all the glory and all the honor. You are so wonderful to me. I could not believe myself today, giving my first shot to a real person. Drawing the eighteen units of insulin was scary. Thank you, Lord, for having Mrs. P. help me. She was so patient with me. It was hard to believe myself after I did it. I also checked blood glucose for a resident for the first time. I was a bit nervous, but I did it! This all happened in the morning. I was surprised with the dressing change. I am really happy with my instructor. I am still gaining confidence and taking each day at a time, and right now I am waiting for more surprises tomorrow. Thank you, Lord, for blessing my day. "This is the day which the Lord hath made; we will rejoice and be glad in it" (Psalm 118: 24 KJV).

September 29, 2006

Lord, I thank you for today. I didn't do much, but I am encouraged. My heart is at peace. Thank you for your love and protection. I am glad that I have been able to touch the lives of many people. Thank you for what is ahead of me, for I know that with your power, I'll make it. Blessed be your name. See me through this weekend, oh Lord. Help me finish the work that is ahead of me; help me in time management, so that I can have time with my family. I pray for my family so that they can understand what I am going through and give me time to study. In Jesus' name, I know I will be able to give shots next Friday. Help me, oh Lord. Let your grace be sufficient for me. In Jesus' name I pray, amen.

God will always give you grace that you need at the right time and for the situation that you are in. "But he said to me, 'My grace is sufficient for you, for my power is made perfect in weakness.' Therefore I will boast all the more gladly about my weaknesses, so that Christ's power may rest on me" (2 Corinthians 12:9)

October 3, 2006

Lord, you are so good and worthy of praise. I lift you up for how far you have helped me. Thank you for helping me cope with everyday life. Sometimes it is hard when I do not pass a test, but your grace has been sufficient. When I am discouraged, you tell me to keep going. I have seen you being my helper. As the days go by, things are becoming harder and harder; I am getting so stressed each day. Lord, I need your help. With you, I know I will make it.

I pray for the instructors. Sometimes I know it is hard for them too. Lord, remember them. Give them joy as they do this work. I pray for my husband, who is always encouraging me and helping me stay with the children, who are patient with me even when I do not have time to play games with them. Thank you, Lord, for those who are praying for me. Lord, bless them. In Jesus' name, amen.

October 13, 2006

Today was my first time to do three tests in one day. It was not easy to decide which one to study for. I did not do well in ATI, but I believe next time I'll make it. It is hard to know where to review, but I know that with God's help, I'll make it. I thank Ms. Y. and Mrs. H. for making the test so easy for us. Help other students to appreciate the instructors. Help me in the remaining time as I study and go to work. Take care of my family. I also need more time with you, Lord. In Jesus' name I pray, amen.

October 17, 2006

Lord, you are worthy to be praised. I lift up your name, the name that is above every name. In this name every knee shall bow and every tongue confess that you are Lord. You know me by my name, and you know what causes stress, and you know my heart. I have been very discouraged and do not know what to do. My heart is not at peace. I have been failing my tests, and I do not understand why. You know better than I do. I try my best to study and to do all that I can. I need your help, oh Lord. Tomorrow is the last test; I do not know what I will get. Help me, oh Lord, to get more than 78, which is the passing mark. Help me as I study. I need your encouragement. Help me, oh Lord, that I'll not be told to leave because of poor grades.

Lord, you are worthy to be praised and to be exalted. As chicks hide in their mom's wings, I am hiding in your wings. Lord, it is so hard for me. I need your help. Help me and give me more grace to be able to continue. I have hope and trust in you, and I know you can fight for me. I thank you, Lord, for you know my future. In Jesus' name, amen. "He will cover you with his feathers, and under his wings you will find refuge; his faithfulness will be your shield and rampart" (Psalm 91:4). "'For I know the plans I have for you,' declares the Lord, 'plans to prosper you and not to harm you, plans to give you hope and a future'" (Jeremiah 29:11).

October 26, 2006

It has taken me almost ten days to write again. Not because I did not have anything to write; it is only because of how busy I have been. I have also been confused because of my grades, but I thank God today that I can smile. After praying for my grade, I got a 96 on my last test, which looked impossible. My loving husband encouraged me and told me it was possible to get a 90. I studied, and at the same time I believed in God. After the test, instead of a 98 I got 100 percent. This was a miracle beyond my understanding. I am still holding on to God's surprises. He is a miracle-working God.

I am also grateful that today is my first day of clinical at the hospital. This is another miracle I have been waiting for. Although I have not done anything yet, I believe God will see me through. He has brought me this far, and I know he will see me through. My prayer is to think positive and to know God is on my side. My prayer is that as I touch the life and body of the patient, there will be a difference. Let the name of the Lord be praised. "For God is not a God of disorder but of peace—as in all the congregations of the saints" (1 Corinthians 14:33).

October 29, 2006

Thank you, Lord, for your love and protection. Your love endures forever, and your mercies are new every morning. It is so good to be alive and talk to you, Lord. I am overwhelmed by your love. Last week was a wonderful week. My first time in clinical was wonderful and enjoyable. I was not very sure about what to expect because the place looked more advanced than a nursing home, but I thank you, Lord, that you helped me be comfortable. For me to get into a clinical setting is a miracle from God. Whatever I do takes God's hand. I am also grateful that I passed both of my tests.

Lord, I pray that you may help me even in this coming week. I cannot make it without you. Help me also in my clinical next week. Help me to be composed, and let your love surround me. Hold me close to you even as I work, take care of my family, and go to school. I need your grace. In Jesus' name I pray, amen.

November 2, 2006

Lord, I thank you. Your loves endures forever. You are wonderful in my life. From everlasting to everlasting, you are God. I thank you for this week. It has not been very easy for me. I had some days that I got discouraged, but I thank you, for you have been on my side. You have taught me to encourage myself in you, oh Lord, just like the way David encouraged himself in the Lord. You still talk to me in Hebrews 13:5, where it says that "you will never leave me nor forsake me." Thank you, Lord, that through the entire crisis in school and clinical you keep telling me to keep going. This is not the time to give up. When I do not understand the material, open my mind that I may understand, Lord. Thank you for helping me pass my exams. On clinical days, help me to be careful in whatever I do. Lord, you are so good to me. As I start this month of November, be with me and help me to succeed. In Jesus' name I thank you and believe.

"But now, this is what the Lord says he who created you, Jacob, he who formed you, Israel: 'Do not fear, for I have redeemed you;

47

I have summoned you by name; you are mine. When you pass through the waters, I will be with you; and when you pass through the rivers, they will not sweep over you. When you walk through the fire, you will not be burned; the flames will not set you ablaze'" (Isaiah 43:1–2).

November 10, 2006

Lord, I thank you for your love and mercy endures forever. It has been a long time since I wrote, but I thank you for your love and protection. Many things have happened, and Lord, you have given me enough grace to bear with each and every situation. God, you have been my comforter. You have used my husband to be my encourager, and I praise you for that. I thank you for using my husband as my support, together with my children.

I have gone through tough times, but I thank you because tough times make me strong, and they do not last forever, but tough people do. Thank you for making me a tough person. Sometimes I do not know how to be tough and I feel like giving up, but your Word says that you shall renew the strength of those who wait upon you. They shall run like eagles and they shall not faint. Help me, Lord, not to faint. Help me not to give up. Sometimes things are so hard for me. I really need your help and somebody to hold on to. I need to hold on to you, Lord. You are so wonderful. From everlasting to everlasting, you are God. Thank you so much in Jesus' name, amen.

"He gives strength to the weary and increases the power of the weak. Even youths grow tired and weary, and young men stumble and fall; but those who hope in the Lord will renew their strength.

They will soar on wings like eagles; they will run and not grow weary, they will walk and not be faint" (Isaiah 40:29–31).

November 14, 2006

Lord, I come to you with thanksgiving in my heart. You are holy and mighty. You are a wonderful God. You care for me in all that I do. Sometimes I feel down and lonely. Sometimes it is even hard for me to understand what I am learning, but I thank you, for you have been with me. This time, Lord, I pray that you will help me because of the test tomorrow. When I try to do it without your help, I fail, but when you intervene, I pass. Help me, Lord, with the respiratory test tomorrow. I have seen you walking with me since I started. The teacher says it will be hard. I need your help to pass this test. Help me to remember all the NCLEX questions. Thank you for your love and for the help you have been offering. In Jesus' name I pray, amen.

November 24, 2006

"If you remain completely silent at this time, relief and deliverance will arise for the Jews from another place, but you and your father's house will perish. Yet who knows whether you have come to the kingdom for such a time as this" (Esther 4:14).

"Oh, how I love you, Jesus, because you first loved me." I thank you for your help. I passed my respiratory test and my diabetes test. Lord, you are so good to me; you are so faithful, Lord. I have started cardiovascular and digestive disorders. They are so hard for me. I have not passed any of the tests so far. I am worried, and I do not know what to do. I am trying to study and memorize, but I am not getting it. I need your help, oh Lord. During Thanksgiving time I am only thinking of the tests ahead of me. The stinking-thinking feelings that I won't make it are coming into my mind. Please, Lord, intervene and refresh my mind that I may remember what I study.

Lord, my desire is to graduate and be a nurse who can help other people. Please, Lord, do not let me down. My family is looking unto me. My enemies are waiting so that I can fail, but I know that with you, all things are possible. Right now I am studying, but I cannot understand most of the things I am studying. So Lord, help me, for I have to go to work tomorrow. I also need you in clinical. I will start doing medications on Friday. I am scared and nervous about that.

Lord, help me. I pray that I may receive favor from Ms. P., and I thank you, Lord, for making her my clinical instructor. I am in this class at this time of the year for a reason and a purpose; it is not by accident. Just as you chose Queen Esther to be the queen for a reason, you have chosen me to be in this class for a reason. Give me confidence in whatever I do. In Jesus' name, amen.

"When Esther's words were reported to Mordecai, he sent back this answer: 'Do not think that because you are in the king's house you alone of all the Jews will escape. For if you remain silent at this time, relief and deliverance for the Jews will arise from another place, but you and your father's family will perish. And who knows but that you have come to your royal position for such a time as this?'" (Esther 4:12–14).

November 27, 2006

Lord, I thank you for allowing me to pass my test. I thank you for answering my prayers. It was not very easy. I was discouraged during Thanksgiving because of not passing three tests, but now I am grateful for your help. Help me not to have stinking thinking. I know with your help and my instructors' help, I will make it. I cannot do without you. You are all powerful, Lord. What you need from me is for me to be obedient and study and believe in you. I thank you, for you are so loving. In Jesus' name I pray. "If you are willing and obedient, you will eat the good things of the land" (Isaiah 1:19). NIV

"Trust in the Lord with all your heart and lean not on your own understanding; in all your ways submit to him, and he will make your paths straight" (Proverbs 3:5–6). Amen.

December 8, 2006

Lord, I love to be in your presence. Thank you for your love and comfort. I thank you for how far you have brought me. I have passed through challenges and difficulties, and sometimes I feel depressed, but I thank you, for you have been on my side. Sometimes it is even hard to get somebody to talk to, but I thank you, for you are always there for me. Clinicals are hard for me, especially when it comes to injection and drugs and mixing insulin, but I thank you, Lord, for you are there to help me. Do not let me down.

I need you, oh Lord, at this time when I feel so down and everything seems to be so hard. Please give me peace and help me out. I need your love and your encouragement. Comfort me at this time when I feel like I am not doing as my instructors want me to do or expect from me. Help me also in my class work. Sometimes I study but do not get good grades. Please help me, Lord. In Jesus' name, amen. "Call to Me and I will answer you and show you great and mighty things, fenced in *and* hidden, which you do not know (do not distinguish and recognize, have knowledge of and understand)" (Jeremiah 33:3 AMP).

December 17, 2006

"This is the day the Lord has made; let us rejoice and be glad in it" (Psalm 118:24). This is the day the Lord has made for me to rejoice and be glad in it. Sometimes it is not easy to rejoice when I am under stress or discouraged. Lord, I thank you for giving me life. I thank you for forgiving my sins. You are God, and beside you there is no other God. You are worthy of praise and honor. Thank you for this time of the year. We are almost celebrating Christmas.

You have brought me this far on my studies. Help me, oh Lord, not to fail or give up. I have five more months remaining. I do not know how to approach these five months, but Lord, you know everything; you are omnipresent. Blessed be your holy name. I am worried about clinical work; it is so challenging and discouraging at times. I need your strength, oh Lord. I need your comfort. Sometimes it is so hard when you do not know what you are doing and feel like you are messing up. Please, Lord, at this time I need you more than before. You have been on my side. I cannot make it without you. I need your love and comfort.

I also thank you for what you have done for my husband. It was a miracle from you that he passed his test. Thank you for many things you have done for us as a family. Bless my children, Joy and Glorious. Help me to teach them your way, oh Lord. In Jesus' name I pray. "Train up a child in the way he should go: and when he is old, he will not depart from it" (Proverbs 22:6 KJV).

December 29, 2006

Lord, I bless your holy name, the name that is above every name. In your name, every knee shall bow and every tongue confess that you are Lord. You are worthy of praise. I just thank you for all that you have done for me and my family. Thank you, Lord, that I passed cardiovascular. It was a scary, difficult term, but with you, oh Lord, I made it through, blessed be your name.

I have five more months. I can't do it without you. I am scared of clinical. I do not know which instructor to get, but Lord, intervene in all my ways. Give me favor to all the instructors, and let your glory be manifested. In all challenges, help me not to give up. I need your strength and your encouragement. Even as I start 2007, Lord, be with me. Let the instructors see something different in me. I humble myself under your mighty hands. Take all my fears, Lord. Once again I thank you for all that you have done. Thank you for seeing my husband through and providing a job for him. As he starts next semester, Lord, help him to pass all his tests. Thank you for all the teachers and students who are willing to help me. I give you all the glory, honor, and majesty.

"Therefore God exalted him to the highest place and gave him the name that is above every name, that at the name of Jesus every knee should bow, in heaven and on earth and under the earth, and every tongue acknowledge that Jesus Christ is Lord, to the glory of God the Father" (Philippians 2:9–11). Amen.

January 5, 2007

Lord, I thank you: another year has started. I am so glad for all your help. I have a few more months to go. Remove all my fears and worries. I was so much longing for January, and I knew that if I got to January, I'd know I could make it. Help me to keep holding on. You are the Lord who changes not. You are exalted among the nations. Thank you for helping me pass the Gastrointestinal (GI) test with a B. It is so encouraging. Help me for the remaining tests I have. I know that with you, all things are possible.

I also thank you for my clinical experience. Last time I was in clinical, I was discouraged. I thought I was not doing so well, but this week I learned that others are still learning, too, and that they do not know everything. I thank you for your help this week in clinical. I have learned a lot. Thank you for controlling my anxiety.

As I go to another floor with a different instructor, I need your help. I pray for favor from you and from the instructor I get. My prayer is that all of us will make it through to graduation. Give me enough energy to study and to remember whenever I am taking my test. I thank you because very soon I will be graduating. Thank you that you are helping me to be confident in myself. I lift you up that you also helped me today to make a call and ask for a blood transfusion. That was awesome. I lift you up, for you are worthy of praise. In Jesus' name I pray, amen.

January 18, 2007

Oh Lord, I thank you for your love that endures forever. You are so good to me. Even when I am messed up, you never let me down. You are my power, my guide, and my strength. Last week I had a very hard weekend. I was very bothered. I shed a lot of tears because of my teacher's comment: she commented in a mean way that I am slow in giving meds. Lord, you are the Creator, and you created me differently from anyone else. That is why I am special; I am fearfully and wonderfully made. I am unique, but my instructor wanted to compare me with other students. I thank you for all that you are doing and what you have done for me. Thank you for giving me peace. Thank you for taking me to a different instructor.

Father, I pray that you may help me. I do not know what to expect tomorrow, but Lord, you know. I am afraid of facing the day tomorrow. I need your help. Do not forsake me, oh Lord. Thank you that today I had a wonderful day. I learned a lot from dialysis, and I thank you for the patient I took care of. You are an awesome God, and your love endures forever.

I have a few months left. I do not know what is ahead of me. I still need you, oh Lord. It is like there is a mountain ahead of me. Help me to climb this mountain. The work you started in me you will come to accomplish. Thank you for giving me a wonderful husband. He has been of great help and encouragement to me. Thank you for my kids; they are really supporting me in prayers. Thank you for the instructors who are waiting for my success. In Jesus' name I pray, amen.

"These things I have spoken unto you, that in me ye might have peace. In the world ye shall have tribulation: but be of good cheer; I have overcome the world" (John 16:33 KJV). "No temptation has overtaken you except what is common to mankind. And God is faithful; he will not let you be tempted beyond what you can bear. But when you are tempted he will also provide a way out so that you can endure it" (1 Corinthians 10:13).

January 23, 2007

Lord, I thank you. I have no words to express my sincere thanks to you. Thank you for how far you have brought me. You saw me through last weekend during clinical. Lord, I am trusting you this week, too. Do not let me down. Give me a good instructor and good students to work with. Thank you, Lord, for you have never failed me or let me down. Please, Lord, see me through this month. As we start a new unit on pediatrics, help me love it and understand it. Protect me from sickness, and help me to face each new day with courage and confidence. When things do not go the way I want, help me to keep trusting in you. Thank you for my husband and children. They are really of great support in this program. Thank you also for the students who are ready to help me whenever I need help. In Jesus' name I pray, amen.

> For this reason, since the day we heard about you, we have not stopped praying for you. We continually ask God to fill you with the knowledge of his will through all the wisdom and understanding that the Spirit gives, so that you may live a life worthy of the Lord and please him in every way: bearing fruit in every good work, growing in the knowledge of God, being strengthened with all power according to his glorious might so that you may have great endurance and patience, and giving joyful thanks to the Father, who has qualified you to share in the inheritance of his holy people in the kingdom of light. For he has rescued us from the dominion of darkness and brought us into the kingdom of the

Son he loves, in whom we have redemption, the forgiveness of sins. (Colossians 1:9–14)

February 5, 2007

Lord, I thank you for all that you have done for me. You are worthy of praise. Thank you for how far you have brought me. It is just with your help, power, and miracles that I'll make it. We have finished the medical-surgical (med-surg) unit, and you helped me to get a B. Thank you, Jesus. We have started another unit, and we have been getting extra credit on attendance and workbook but now this extra credit has been discontinued. Help me to pass even without extra credit. Lord, for the remaining units I need you, oh Lord. Help me not to be the next one thrown out. Five students have already left. It is so sad, oh Lord. I need you for the remaining months. It seems to be hard, but I thank you because there is nothing impossible with you. Give me techniques for how to study. Open my understanding that I may understand the teachers. Let the Devil be ashamed with this whole program. Oh Lord, I want to see you. In Jesus' name I pray. The Devil is still under my feet. "You have armed me with strength for the battle; you have subdued my enemies under my feet" (2 Samuel 22:40 NLT).

February 22, 2007

Thank you, oh Lord, for your love and for your concern about my life. I exalt you, oh Lord, for you are worthy and wonderful. Thank you for being the Creator of everything, and thank you for creating me in your own image. I exalt you, oh Lord. I bless you, oh Lord, for what you have done in my life and for being so wonderful to my family. Thank you for Lenard, Joy, and Glorious. I lift you up.

I pray, Lord, that you may help me with neurology. My desire is to pass, oh Lord. It seems hard for me, but Lord, I know everything is possible for those who believe. Help me to pass, oh Lord. I am trying my best, and I leave everything else to you. Help me in maternity. It is hard and there are a lot of things to do, but I thank you, Lord, because you will see me through. I bless your name even for clinical that today I will not be stressed. I feel comfortable in the mental health unit. For the remaining months, oh Lord, I need you. In Jesus' name I pray. "Jesus looked at them and said, 'With man this is impossible, but not with God; all things are possible with God'" (Mark 10:27).

March 15, 2007

I bless your name, for you are worthy to be praised. You are wonderful in my life. Worthy is your name. I have seen you doing wonders in my life. When I was almost giving up, you were there to encourage me and to tell me to keep holding on. You are a wonderful God. You are my mighty Savior.

My week has been good. I thank you, Lord, that I passed in neurology. These are all your miracles. I have confidence in you, and I know, oh Lord, that I am going to make it.

Today was not a good day for me in clinical. It was so tense, and the instructor was so unkind. My heart felt so down and lonely. Lord, I need you. I have a lot to do this weekend, and without you I cannot make it. For the two days remaining with the same instructor, I will need you, oh Lord. I am so uncomfortable in that place and also with the group. Lift my spirit up, oh Lord. I do not know why that instructor doesn't like me, but oh Lord, you know why, and your love surrounds me. I do not have any grudge against her. Give me a happy ending as I leave her this Friday. Let your name be glorified, oh Lord. For the time remaining, I am still waiting for you. I still need your help. I exalt you. In Jesus' name I pray.

"He says, 'Be still, and know that I am God; I will be exalted among the nations, will be exalted in the earth'" (Psalm 46:10).

During this period of time a miracle happened and one of the instructors noticed that I was not getting along well with my clinical instructor. Before the clinical day came, the Lord performed a miracle and I was removed from this instructors' group. God answers prayers.

"Even though I walk through the darkest valley I will fear no evil, for you are with me; your rod and your staff, they comfort me" (Psalm 23:4). "No one will be able to stand up against you all the days of your life. As I was with Moses, so I will be with you; I will never leave you nor forsake you. Be strong and courageous because you will lead these people to inherit the land I swore to their forefathers to give them. Be strong and very courageous. Be careful to obey all the law my servant Moses gave you; do not turn from it to the right or to the left, that you may be successful wherever you go" (Joshua 1:5–7).

"So do not fear, for I am with you; do not be dismayed, for I am your God. I will strengthen you and help you; I will uphold you with my righteous right hand" (Isaiah 41:10). "Give all your worries and cares to God, for he cares about you" (1 Peter 5:7 NLT).

May 24, 2007

But now, this is what the Lord says—he who created you, Jacob, he who formed you, Israel: "Do not fear, for I have redeemed you; I have summoned you by name; you are mine. When you pass through the waters, I will be with you; and when you pass through the rivers, they will not sweep over you. When you walk through the fire, you will not be burned; the flames will not set you ablaze. For I am the Lord your God, the Holy One of Israel, your Savior; I give Egypt for your ransom, Cush and Seba in your stead. Since you are precious and honored in my sight, and because I love you, I will give people in exchange for you, nations in exchange for your life. Do not be afraid, for I am with you; I will bring your children from the east and gather you from the west. I will say to the north, 'Give them up!' and to the south, 'Do not hold them back.' Bring my sons from afar and my daughters from the ends of the earth—everyone who is called by my name, whom I created for my glory, whom I formed and made." Lead out those who have eyes but are blind, who have ears but are deaf. All the nations gather together and the peoples assemble. Which of their gods foretold this and proclaimed to us the former things? Let them bring in their witnesses to prove they were right, so that others may hear and say, "It is true." "You are my witnesses," declares the Lord, "and my servant whom I have chosen, so that you may know and believe me and understand that I am he. Before me no god was formed, nor will there be one after me. I, even I am the Lord, and apart from me there is no savior. I have revealed and saved and proclaimed—I, and not some foreign god among you. You are my witnesses," declares the Lord, "that I am God. Yes, and from ancient days I am he. No one can deliver out of my hand. When I act, who can reverse it?" (Isaiah 43:1–13)

CHAPTER 6

THANKFUL BEYOND WORDS

I am so thankful to God beyond words. "When you pass through the water, I will be with you; and when you pass through the rivers, they will not sweep over you. When you walk through the fire, you will not be burned; the flames will not set you ablaze." (Isaiah 43:2)

I did not write anything the whole of April. Things have been hectic; I have been busy with homework, studying for the tests, and spending time with my family. April went flying by, and before I knew it, it was already May. God is faithful! It has been more than a month since I last wrote about what is going on. I have passed through hard times. I have cried, and I have questioned whether I'll make it. Sometimes I have gone through frustration, but all in all I have seen you, oh Lord. Your wonderful hand has been upon me. Your Word tells me, "Come to me, all who labor and are heavy laden, and I will give you rest" (Matthew 11:28). I have seen rest in Jesus Christ.

The Devil has tried hard to fight with me about school, but I have seen God on my side. I am more than a conqueror. My thanks go to my instructors, who have always been with me in times of stress. Lord, this is a very special day for me. I cannot explain my joy because my joy is beyond words. I did not know that a day would come when I'd say, "This is my last day of clinical." Today is the day—hallelujah. Thank you, Lord for all those people I have touched in the hospital. Thank you for all those nurses who were willing to help. I also pray for other students who went through the same struggle as I did. Lord, as I look forward to the pinning and graduation, I pray that you will be with me. Help me even after I graduate to be able to touch the lives of other people. Remove every fear and worry, and grant me a job according to your will.

It has not been easy to go through this class, but with you, Lord, I can stand with a testimony. Lord, manifest yourself in whatever is ahead of me and your name will be glorified. In Jesus' name I pray, amen.

For the spirit God gave us does not make us timid, but gives us power, love and self discipline. (1Tim 1:7)Sometimes we go through frustrations and ask ourselves, where is our God? God is right there where you are, closer than the air you breathe. He is in control of every situation. He always wants us to win in whatever we do according to his will. "Let us then approach God's throne of grace with confidence, so that we may receive mercy and find grace to help us in our time of need" (Hebrews 4:16). I have decided to approach God's throne with confidence. Many people go to God with fear of punishment because of the way they were brought up in their Christian life. When I was growing up, I knew God as a father who always says, "Do not do this," "Do not do that," and I grew up with fear. Later in life, I learned that God is not only a God of punishment but a loving father. Other people compare God with their fathers, and if their fathers were harsh, they think God is the same way, but I want to tell you that God is love and he wants us to succeed in life. He wants us to go to him with confidence.

We need to approach God and ask for mercy and grace for every day. "No, in all these things we are more than conquerors through him who loved us" (Romans 8:37). It is because of God's love that I have been able to accomplish this dream. I can say that I am more than a conqueror because I have already conquered. It might not look like a battle to go through studies, but it was a huge battle for me. I had to fight spiritually and pray to achieve my goal.

CHAPTER 7

JUNE 2007

"For my thoughts are not your thoughts, neither are your ways my ways," declares the Lord. "As the heavens are higher than the earth, so are my ways higher than your ways and my thoughts than your thoughts" (Isaiah 55:8–9).

The pinning ceremony is here. Everyone is excited, waiting for the big ceremony. God is a miracle-working God. There is no mountain I cannot climb when I am with Jesus. God is in control of my life, he is still on the throne, and after all this, he is going to open a job for me according to his will. His ways are very different from people's ways and even from my way. After this, I know I have a hurdle to jump, which is my NCLEX, and I know God is going to see me through. I take this opportunity to thank everyone for all their kindness and support; I am now a licensed practical nurse applicant. It is unbelievable.

> Give thanks to the Lord, for he is good; his love endures forever. Let Israel say: "His love endures forever." Let the house of Aaron say: "His love endures forever." Let those who fear the Lord say:

"His love endures forever." When hard pressed, I cried to the Lord; he brought me into a spacious place. The Lord is with me; I will not be afraid. What can mere mortals do to me? The Lord is with me; he is my helper. I look in triumph on my enemies. It is better to take refuge in the Lord than to trust in humans. It is better to take refuge in the Lord than to trust in princes. All the nations surrounded me, but in the name of the Lord I cut them down. They surrounded me on every side, but in the name of the Lord I cut them down. They swarmed around me like bees, but they were consumed as quickly as burning thorns; in the name of the Lord I cut them down. I was pushed back and about to fall, but the Lord helped me. The Lord is my strength and my defense; he has become my salvation. Shouts of joy and victory resound in the tents of the righteous: "The Lord's right hand has done mighty things! The Lord's right hand is lifted high; the Lord's right hand has done mighty things!" I will not die but live, and will proclaim what the Lord has done. The Lord has chastened me severely, but he has not given me over to death. Open for me the gates of the righteous; I will enter and give thanks to the Lord. This is the gate of the Lord through which the righteous may enter. I will give you thanks, for you answered me; you have become my salvation. The stone the builders rejected has become the cornerstone; the Lord has done this, and it is marvelous in our eyes. The Lord has done it this very day; let us rejoice today and be glad. Lord, save us! Lord, grant us success! Blessed is he who comes in the name of the Lord. From the house of the Lord we bless you. The Lord is God, and he has made his light shine on us. With boughs in hand, join in the festal procession up to the horns of the altar. You are my God, and I will praise you; you are my God, and I will exalt you. Give thanks to the LORD, for he is good; his love endures forever. (Psalm 118)

I am having a time of thanksgiving; it is an emotional time after feeling like a heavy burden has been lifted from my shoulders. I feel like the way a mother feels after delivering a child. I am full of joy and cannot avoid crying. I praise my God, and exalt him for bringing my dream to reality.

Prayer

Thank you, Lord, because this has not happened with my own power. You have brought light to shine in my life. I will praise you for your goodness and mercy. I will praise you for saving me and granting me success. Thank you for what you have done this day. I cannot hold back my joy. What you have done in my life is marvelous in my eyes, and I cannot hold back my excitement. I was about to fall, but you held me up, just like the way Aaron and Hur held Moses' arms and the Israelites won the battle, you held me up and I won the battle, oh Lord of my salvation. "When Moses' hands grew tired, they took a stone and put it under him and he sat on it. Aaron and Hur held his hands up—one on one side, one on the other—so that his hands remained steady till sunset" (Exodus 17:12).

I have learned to trust in you and not to take refuge in humans. You have been with me and have been my helper in this journey. I am thanking you, for you are my God and your love endures forever. I am going to continue to trust you even for my future. In Jesus' name I pray, amen.

CHAPTER 8

Do Not Despise a Humble Beginning

After the pinning and graduation I started to pray for God to open a job opportunity for me. I also started to prepare myself for the big national exam, NCLEX. I applied for a job in two different places. At that time, these two places were hiring people without licenses, but at present a nurse is required to have a license to be hired. So I was ready to start the job and at the same time, study for my test. I wanted to work in a hospital on a medical-surgical floor or with psychiatric patients. I applied for a job at a psychiatric hospital, but I still had my fears. During my prayers I told God, "Whoever calls me first, I will know this is where you want me to be," but at the same time I had my will and desires.

I wanted the hospital to call me first, but to my surprise the psychiatric hospital called me first. I wrestled with this and tried to tell God, "No way; this cannot be true." So I did another trial and told God I would wait for the hospital to call me. I would give them two weeks, and if they had not called me in two weeks, I would go ahead with the job offer at the psychiatric hospital. Two weeks went by fast, and the hospital never called. I went ahead and took the job offer at the psychiatric hospital. When I started, I had to take an orientation class for three weeks, and on my second week of orientation, the hospital called, offering me a job. I said no because I had already committed myself to the psychiatric hospital job.

I am so glad that I took this job at the psychiatric hospital; it was the best decision I have ever made. This is my sixth year in the job, and when I look back, I thank God that he allowed me to take this opportunity to work with psychiatric patients. I have learned a lot from the patients and my coworkers, and I know that God has placed me there for a reason and a purpose. Sometimes it is hard to understand God's will, but it is important to let God's will be done in our lives. This doesn't mean that there are no challenges in this job. I face challenges now and then, but God's grace has been sufficient for me every day. As nurses it does not matter where we work, there will be challenges most of the time, but the most important thing is to trust in Jesus.

I was also able to study for my boards with the help of Assessment Technologies Institute (ATI), and I failed on my first attempt. I was very discouraged because I was demoted at my work and I had to work as a nurse's aide for more than a month before retaking my boards. My mind started telling me maybe I was not meant to be a nurse. I started to question why I had put all my energy into this. I almost gave up, but I had to pull myself up. I decided to study again, and with God's help I passed the second time.

If you have failed in your boards, do not give up. Yes, I say, "Do not give up." God is the God of first, second, third, and fourth chances. Lift your hopes up and tell yourself you can do it, and God will see you through. Start having positive thoughts about yourself.

If I passed, you can pass too. Keep trusting in God and do not quit. Stop listening to the voice of the enemy, speak positively to yourself, and God will see you through.

After I passed my National Council Licensure Examination (NCLEX) I took a one-year break from school to spend time with my family before deciding to go back to school to become a registered nurse. First I had to take prerequisites, which took me almost a year. Prerequisites were also a challenge, especially since English is my second language. I had to depend on God, and sometimes I asked myself whether I would make it. After finishing the prerequisites, I was accepted into the nursing program, which was also a challenge but was much better than the LPN program. I was already familiar with the terminologies, which made it even easier. The challenges of the RN program were not as bad as what I had gone through with the LPN program. I am now a registered nurse and still working with psychiatric patients at the same hospital.

After I got my RN associate's degree, I took another yearlong break to spend time with my family and cerebrate the accomplishment that the Lord had given me. Then I decided to go back to school and further my education, so I am enrolled in a university to obtain my bachelor of science degree in nursing. It has still not been easy, but with God's grace, it has been possible. I am always depending on God to see me through. I have come to learn that if you commit your mind and heart unto God, you can succeed. Do not despise the humble beginning, because the Lord will always bless the work of our hands.

> Gideon replied, "If now I have found favor in your
> eyes, give me a sign that it is really you talking to me.

Please do not go away until I come back and bring my offering and set it before you." And the Lord said, "I will wait until you return." Gideon went inside, prepared a young goat, and from an ephah of flour he made bread without yeast. Putting the meat in a basket and its broth in a pot, he brought them out and offered them to him under the oak. The angel of God said to him, "Take the meat and the unleavened bread, place them on this rock, and pour out the broth." And Gideon did so. Then the angel of the Lord touched the meat and the unleavened bread with the tip of the staff that was in his hand. Fire flared from the rock, consuming the meat and the bread. And the angel of the Lord disappeared. When Gideon realized that it was the angel of the Lord, he exclaimed, "Alas, Sovereign Lord! I have seen the angel of the Lord face to face!" (Judges 6:17–22)

Before I took my job, I did like Gideon because I wanted to know exactly where the Lord wanted me to be. It is important to check if we are doing God's will. Hezekiah wanted to know if it was God who said that he would receive his healing. Sometimes God speaks to us through his Word, through prayer, through other people, in our spirit, and through signs. Before making any important decision, it is good to pray, listen to the spirit of God speaking to our hearts, and read the Word of God.

"Who dares despise the day of small things, since the seven eyes of the Lord that range throughout the earth will rejoice when they see the chosen capstone in the hand of Zerubbabel?" (Zachariah 4:10).

I am so thankful that I took my LPN course very seriously; it was a step toward where I am today. If I had despised the course of study, maybe I could not have reached the point where I am today. It was a very humble beginning and a great foundation in my career life. I encourage all students not to despise the humble beginning. Maybe you are taking a certified nursing class, which I also took before I became an LPN. Do not despise it, because it is going to be a step up toward a better future for you.

CHAPTER 9

WHY DO YOU SIT THERE UNTIL YOU DIE?

Most of the time after failing in life, most of us sit in self-pity, not wanting to try again. Some people isolate themselves after failing. It is hard to think of attempting to do something again after failing. But many people fail in life the first time, and they try again. Maybe you have failed multiple times. I just want to encourage you to try again. Do not sit on self-pity until you die. Rise up, and God will see you through. Life is too short for you to sit in self-pity and depression. Rise up because your light has come.

Four Lepers Changed the City.

> Now there were four men with leprosy at the entrance of the city gate. They said to each other, "Why stay here until we die? If we say, 'We'll go into the city'—the famine is there, and we will die. And if we stay here, we will die. So let's go over to the camp of the Syrians and surrender. If they spare us,

we live; if they kill us, then we die." At dusk they got up and went to the camp of the Syrians. When they reached the edge of the camp, no one was there, for the Lord had caused the Syrians to hear the sound of chariots and horses and a great army, so that they said to one another, "Look, the king of Israel has hired the Hittite and Egyptian kings to attack us!" So they got up and fled in the dusk and abandoned their tents and their horses and donkeys. They left the camp as it was and ran for their lives. The men who had leprosy had reached the edge of the camp entered one of the tents and ate and drank. Then they took silver, gold and clothes, and went off and hid them. They returned and entered another tent and took some things from it and hid them also. Then they said to each other, "What we're doing is not right. This is a day of good news and we are keeping it to ourselves. If we wait until daylight, punishment will overtake us. Let's go at once and report this to the royal palace." (2 Kings 7:3–9)

There was a famine in Samaria, and people were starving and eating their own babies. There were these four lepers outside the city gate. They could not go in because there were enemies, and outside they were dying of hunger. They decided to go inside the city no matter what happened to them. They said to one another, "Why do we sit here until we die? If we stay here, we will die of hunger, and if we go inside, we will be killed, but we might get something to eat." They decided to go inside. My friend, why do you sit there until you die? What is preventing you from receiving your miracle? What is preventing you from getting into your destiny? Is it bitterness, pride, financial struggle? What is preventing you from taking your NCLEX one more time? Is it self-pity? Do not sit there until you die. What kind of situation are you in? Are you surrounded with famine? Are you in fear of going inside? When you are sitting where you are, what do you see? Do you see yourself as more than a conqueror? Do you see yourself as gifted? Do you see yourself as someone who can make a difference in the world? Do you see yourself as anointed of God?

See yourself the way God sees you. God doesn't see you as a failure, as someone who cannot make it in life. You have to start confessing things in your life that you want to acquire and have an "I can do it" attitude. Write down, "I can pass my exams. I can pass NCLEX." Say this every morning. Write it everywhere you can see, and God will see your determination. God has blessed you with heavenly blessings. He did not create you to be a failure; he has created you to be a winner, but you have to say it to yourself.

These lepers stood up and started walking. The Lord made their footsteps sound like a mighty army, and the enemies ran for their lives. There was food inside, and they started eating. They refused to stay outside although they were considered outcast. Sometimes you need to refuse where people put you. People saw these four lepers as outcasts, but that is not how God saw them. You need to refuse to be a failure, if this is the label you have been given. You do not have to accept whatever the Devil throws at you.

They told one another, "If we stay here, we die; if we go inside, we die, but why stay here until we die?" They decided to risk their lives by going inside. How long have you been sitting outside with your problems, with your gifts because you are worried about risking your life? God is looking for those people who pray bold prayers, those who are ready to risk their lives for something new to happen. They knew they were not supposed to be inside, but they risked anyway. Are you ready to risk like these lepers? You are not considered outcast. They were, but God multiplied their steps so that they sounded like a big army. Can you imagine a leper God multiplying their steps? If God can do it for lepers, he can do it for you. He is not a respecter of any persons.

Do not sit there until you die. Take a step of faith and go inside. There is a miracle inside, there is food inside, there are blessings inside, there is healing inside. You are going to change someone's life if you go inside. These four lepers changed the situation in Samaria. People were starving, dying, eating their own babies, but because of the four lepers, the whole of Samaria had food. You are gifted and you can change your city.

Do you know that God can use you to change someone's life after you go inside, discover the blessings and receive them, and then pass them on to someone else? Do you know the potential you have? Do you know the power that God has put in you? What you need to do is refuse to sit where you are until you die. Do not get used to that normal life without expecting a change or a surprise. The lepers did not just eat by themselves; they went and told the gatekeepers. When these lepers informed the gatekeepers, the gatekeepers went and told the king. The king woke up from sleep and started to negotiate with the gatekeepers, trying to figure out what had happened.

Can you imagine four lepers making the king wake up from sleep? Then the king sent chariots with horses to go and see what was going on. Your prayer and determination can wake the king from sleep and make him look at the welfare of the city or country. The economy of Samaria changed; the food was sold very cheap just because of the four lepers who refused to sit where they were until they died. Your potential can change the economy of the country. What you need to do is rise up and see the glory of God. The Bible says in 2 Chronicles 7:14, "If my people, who are called by my name, will humble themselves and pray and seek my face and turn from their wicked ways, then I will hear from heaven, and I will forgive their sin and will heal their land."

Do not expect anything good to happen if you are not getting into agreement with God. God does not use the strong, he doesn't use the wealthy; he uses the weak and the ones who are available. *He used Nehemiah to build the walls of Jerusalem; Nehemiah was just a cupbearer. He used Gideon, who came from the minority tribe, and he used Moses, who was taking care of sheep. God can use you more than you think, to change your life and to change someone else's life.*

I read about this boy who had a withered hand and leg. He was lonely at school. He never smiled, and other students did not want to relate with him. One of the teachers noticed this boy and decided to say hello to him every morning. After a few months, this boy wrote a letter to the teacher to thank her for greeting him. This teacher changed this boy's perspective. You never know what you can do; something small can change someone's life. Do you have a friend who is struggling at school? You can change his or her life through prayer and encouragement. Take some extra time to help somebody with homework.

When I was young, I used to work in a quarry, beating stones into smaller stones for building. Every Saturday, the stones were measured with something like a tin bucket, and we were paid by the owner of the quarry. It was a very hard job for someone my age, but many children in the area did this for food and clothing. When I went to high school, I decided I was not going to do this anymore. I remember telling my mom, "I am done with beating stones" and "I will never beat them again." My mom thought it was a joke. She asked me, "What are you going to do during the holidays?" I said, "I will find other things to do," and do you know, that became my last day of beating stones.

Maybe I would have done that all my life if I had not taken the step of using my mouth to say, "I will not do it again." God opened other opportunities for me during holidays. Even today I know people I used to beat stones with, and they are still beating them. Maybe I would be beating stones even today if I had not taken that bold step. Rise up, and refuse to sit there until you die. Where are you sitting? What are you doing now that you don't like doing? Take a step of faith and confess the things you want to do. These four lepers took a step of faith and decided not to sit there until they died. There is no way you can chase the enemy if you are outside. You have to get in where the enemy is. God will protect you from getting hurt because he will see your faith and determination.

The lepers had deformities, but God multiplied their steps so that they sounded like a huge army. When you take a step of faith, God will open a way for you. You do not have to wait until the Lord opens a way; you have to do it by faith, and when God sees your faith, he will open another way for you. Maybe these lepers had excuses about what they could not do because of their weaknesses, but they all decided to go in. You need to make a decision about what you are doing with your life. Life is too short. Do not sit there until you die. Do something for the kingdom of God. "Cast thy bread upon the waters: for thou shalt find it after many days. Give a portion to seven, and also to eight; for thou knowest not what evil shall be upon the earth" (Ecclesiastes 11:1–2 KJV). When you do something for the kingdom of God, it is like you are casting the bread upon the water, and when you are in need, you will be able to find it.

Most of the time we wait for the Lord to open a way first, without taking a step of faith. It works in the opposite manner. You have to take a step first, and then the Lord will open a way. The Israelites took a step of faith when they stepped into the water, and the Lord parted the water. The three Hebrew boys went into the fire, and Jesus went into the fire afterward. Daniel went into the den of lions before the Lord could shut the mouth of the lion. I am not telling you to be careless with your life, but you have to look at the situation you are in and say, "That is enough, Satan. I am not going to go through this anymore." If you are sick physically or emotionally, do not start preparing to die but prepare to live. What do you need in your life? Start confessing about it like you have it, and God will bring it your way.

There was this girl I knew. In her tribe, her name meant "hardworking". In the school system where she attended, children used to get numbers; for example, if the class had a total of forty students, number one was the best and number forty was the worst. There were no A, B, C grades then, so the child with the highest marks was considered number one. She was not a smart girl, so on every report card, she was the last number, and the students called her names. She was always last in her class and kept repeating every grade, with no improvement. Kids could start school and overtake her because she was not promoted to higher classes. She would stay in one class for about three years, and eventually she got older and had to quit going to school.

During this time, I felt bad that kids called her names, but I never thought about the effect it had on her life. No one said anything positive to her to change her situation, and she had to live all her life without education. Being a child, she did not know any better about speaking for herself, and maybe her parents did not know either or even themselves know the importance of education because many parents in the area were not educated. Can you imagine if anyone had spoken positive words to her? Maybe her life would not have turned out the way it did, especially with her name meaning "hardworking." She just needed a release of blessing to be able to work hard like her name meant.

Maybe you are gifted in speaking words of encouragement and support to people. Do not sit on that gift until you die. Parents, you need to speak to your children; you need to tell them they cannot sit there with bad grades until they die. Tell them they can do better, and make a difference in their lives. God is expecting you to speak positive words to a child and speak positive words to those around you. Change someone's perspective. Especially when you change the life of a child, you never know whom that child will become.

I never thought I was a strong person until I came to the United States. People who leave their country and go to other countries are strong people. The culture shock, the differences, the language, leaving friends and family—just to mention a few things—are not easy. After I got here and was able to fight all the emotional and spiritual battles, I knew I was a strong person, but I came to learn how strong I am when one of my bosses told me, "You are a very strong woman." She never knew what difference she brought into my life, but she changed my perspective, especially because her words came from a person with more authority than I had.

God is telling you how strong you are—stronger than even the lepers—and you can change the world. Do not sit there feeling sorry for yourself, because you have potential. Help that sick, depressed person change his or her situation; speak hope to those who are hopeless, and help them get inside where they can receive their miracle. Help that person with cancer or back pain, and let him or her know there is hope in Jesus. Help your friends, children, parents, and other family members get inside and receive the blessings of the Lord. Let them know that they are just as important as the four lepers, and that God used the four lepers to change the situation in a city.

Peter Heals a Lame Beggar

One day Peter and John were going up to the temple at the time of prayer at three in the afternoon. Now a man who was lame from birth was being carried to the temple gate called Beautiful, where he was put every day to beg from those going into the temple courts. When he saw Peter and John about to enter, he asked them for money. Peter looked straight at him, as did John. Then Peter said, "Look at us!" So the man gave them his attention, expecting to get something from them. Then Peter said, "Silver or gold I do not have, but what I do have I give you. In the name of Jesus Christ of Nazareth, walk." Taking him by the right hand, he helped him up, and instantly the man's feet and ankles became strong. He jumped to his feet and began to walk. Then he went with them into the temple courts, walking and jumping, and praising God. When all the people saw him walking and praising God, they recognized him as the same man who used to sit begging at the temple gate called Beautiful, and they were filled with wonder and amazement at what had happened to him.

Peter Speaks to the Onlookers

While the man held on to Peter and John, all the people were astonished and came running to them in the place called Solomon's Colonnade. When Peter saw this, he said to them: "Fellow Israelites, why does this surprise you? Why do you stare at us as if by our own power or godliness we had made this man walk?" (Acts 3:1–12)

There was a man at the beautiful gate begging for alms. Some history books say that he was in his forties. He was born lame, and although I do not know how long he had been brought to this beautiful gate before his miracle happened, I do know it was a long time. He was used to this kind of life and was expecting to get money from those people who were going into the temple. The reason he was put at this beautiful gate is that whoever put him there knew that people who were going to the synagogue had compassion. There was also a kind of money exchange in this area. This day was like his usual day, and as was his routine, he was waiting to get some money. He asked Peter and John for money. Peter and John told him, "Look at us." They told him to look at them because in his inferiority, he looked down and could not look them in the eye. They told him, "Silver and gold we have none, but in the name of Jesus Christ, rise up and walk."

This man had never been inside the temple because he was considered an outcast, but his time came and he was able to enter. Jesus is saying to you, "Look at me. I am ready to perform a miracle in your life." Peter and John had no silver or gold, but they had the power of the almighty God to be able to help this lame man walk. You do not have to sit at the beautiful gate doing your normal things until you die. Jesus is telling you, "Look at me." It doesn't matter how beautiful the gate looks; Jesus want you to get inside the temple. You might be sitting in a gate of depression, emotional stress, poverty, unforgiveness, or unworthiness, or sitting on your dreams, but God is saying to you, "Look at me." You do not have to sit there until you die. Jesus is coming unto your way. Your situation might be looking like it is lame. You might be looking like the four lepers. Jesus wants you to get inside and enjoy his blessings. You have been sitting there for a long time. It is time to get up and walk. It is time to get inside the temple and start praising God. The Lord wants to change your situation. Do not tell him stories. People are going to be surprised when they see what happens in your life, just as the onlookers were surprised after they saw this lame man. After you pass your exams, "onlookers" will be surprised, wondering how you passed them. Just tell them it was not by your power but that you passed because of the power of the almighty God.

CONCLUSION

I f I made it through, you can make it, too, through determination and prayer and speaking positively about yourself. "The tongue has the power of life and death and those who love it will eat its fruit" (Proverbs 18:12).Whatever you speak about yourself you will bring to pass because there is power in your tongue. I remember my dad had a gallbladder problem and had surgery. After the operation, he started saying he wanted to die. Gallbladder surgery was not serious enough to cause his death, but he confessed what he wanted. A few weeks after the surgery, the sutures came out. I do not know how, but after they came out, he tried to put his hands on the wound and the area became infected. He was admitted to the hospital and continued saying, "I just want to die," and after a month or so, he died.

What do I want to show you? You are the one who can say what you want. My dad called death unto his life, and he got it because of the power of his mouth. Do you want to pass your test, exams, NCLEX? Keep speaking positively about what you want, and God will bring it to pass. You are the only person who can bring success to your life.

As I said in the beginning, I had wanted to be a nurse since I was young, and I almost missed my opportunity because of fear.

Fear makes us believe something that is not true as if it will happen. You might be fearful of going back to school, fearful of sitting for your NCLEX, fearful of failing because your mind thinks you will fail. Replace fear with faith because faith is the substance of things hoped for. We need to have faith in ourselves to conquer fear in our life. The Devil will try to tell you that you cannot make it. He is a liar. The Bible says, "The thief comes only to steal kill and destroy. I came that they may have life, and have it abundantly" (John 10:10 NRSV). God wants you to have life in fullness, but the Devil is a liar. He tried to tempt Jesus, telling him, "It is written." He will try to use and twist the Word of God by telling you, "It is written."

In the garden of Eden, God said to Adam, "You may freely eat of every tree of the garden, but the tree of the knowledge of good and evil you shall not eat, for in the day you eat of it you shall die" (Genesis 2:16–17 NRSV). Adam and Eve were told they could eat from all the trees except the Tree of Knowledge of Good and Evil, but this old serpent, the Devil, went to Eve and said, "Did God say you shall not eat from any tree of the garden?" (Genesis 3:1 NRSV). Eve knew very well what the Lord had said, but the serpent tried to trick her. He is the same old serpent, the Devil, who will try to convince you that you cannot make it.

God always gives us free will. He will continue to give you free will of choosing him, believing and trusting in him even when there is no way. The Bible says he will create a way where there is no way. There might be no way when you try to look with your physical eyes, but the things that we see are temporary, and things that we cannot see are permanent. Right now you cannot see yourself passing that NCLEX, but use your spiritual eyes and trust in the unseen. Do not let the enemy deceive you and tell you that you were not created to become a nurse. Even after I received my license as a registered nurse, the Devil tried to put me down in some issue at my work. He tried to tell me I am not good enough, but I have decided to stand firm and tell him, "Get behind me, Satan, you have no authority over me and you are a liar."

FINAL THOUGHTS

I Will Be with You

God told Joshua, "I will be with you, and my final thoughts to you are that God will be with you no matter how hard it is. Trust in him and he will see you through.

After the death of Moses the servant of the Lord, the Lord said to Joshua son of Nun, Moses' aide: "Moses my servant is dead. Now then, you and all these people, get ready to cross the Jordan River into the land I am about to give to them—to the Israelites. I will give you every place where you set your foot, as I promised Moses. Your territory will extend from the desert to Lebanon, and from the great river, the Euphrates—all the Hittite country—to the Mediterranean Sea in the west. No one will be able to stand against you all the days of your life. As I was with Moses, so I will be with you; I will never leave you nor forsake you. Be strong and courageous, because you will lead these people to inherit the land I swore to their ancestors to give them. "Be strong and very courageous. Be careful to obey all the law my servant Moses gave you; do not turn from it to the right or to the left, that you may be successful wherever you go. Keep this Book of the Law always on your lips; meditate on it day and night, so that you may be careful to do everything written in it. Then you will be prosperous and successful. Have I not commanded you? Be strong and courageous. Do not be afraid; do not be discouraged, for the Lord your God will be with you wherever you go." (Joshua 1:1–9)

It is not easy to tell someone, "I will be with you." Most of the time we want to be with someone, but when things get tough, we see ourselves withdrawing. Not that we want to withdraw, but it gets hard for us because we are human. Even Peter told Jesus he would be with him, but Jesus told him, "Before the cock crows, you will deny me three times." Jesus knows how hard it is for us to be with someone when things get tough. It is also very hard to trust ourselves when things are hard.

Joshua's new job consisted of leading about two million people in a strange land—not only leading the people, but conquering the land. Ahead of him was the first challenge: the Jordan River. The land was occupied, but God wanted the Israelites to take over. God has called us to inherit his promises, but there is someone holding our promises. We need to fight to get what God has for us. Joshua walked with Moses. He knew how hard it was to lead the Israelites, but God promised to be with him. This was also a hard time for Joshua because he had just been mourning the powerful leader

Moses' death, but if God is the one who called you, he will be with you. This does not mean that things are going to be easy, but in difficulties, he will be the source of encouragement. He has said he will never leave you or forsake you.

God will always keep his promise and his work going. We are the people God has chosen to make sure his work continues. The Lord has called you in some way. Maybe you are a singer, an intercessor, or someone who always talks to those who are lonely or always makes someone feel good. Maybe you are an encourager, or maybe you go the extra mile to do something that no one else at your work wants to do. We are all called to make God's work continue. You are the one I am speaking to, that the Lord will be with you. Do not be discouraged, and do not give up. People may not see what you are doing, but God is always looking, and he knows exactly what you are doing. In due time he will pay you back if you don't faint. As you continue doing God's work, the Lord will be with you.

Joshua had seen God being with Moses, so when God told him, "I will be with you," he had confidence that surely God would be with him. Joshua saw God providing manna from heaven, he saw God providing water from a rock, he saw God providing a bronze serpent and whoever looked at it was healed, so he knew that whatever God said, that is what he meant. Do you have confidence in God? Do you know for sure that God will be with you? He also told Joshua, "I will not leave you or forsake you," and this is still the same God we serve. He will never leave us or forsake us. If he has promised to be with us in difficult times, he will carry us through.

As a leader, Joshua did not find it easy, but God told him to be strong and courageous. God knew that Joshua would face difficult situations and obstacles, and that is why he told him to be strong and courageous. Whether you are a minister, a leader, a teacher of the Word, or someone else, you sometimes face very difficult situations that leave you feeling confused and wondering if God is still there. But I am telling you as the Lord told Joshua, be strong and courageous. There are often times when I need to be strong and courageous to continue with my day-to-day life. Sometimes the battles are challenging and I wonder if I am going to overcome, but the Lord has told me that he will be with me. I am more than a conqueror.

Maybe there are obstacles in your life, or maybe you are facing situations that you do not know how to solve. Maybe sometimes you feel like crying or giving up. I want to let you know that God is telling you, "I will be with you." Maybe someone has done something that is so painful that you cannot let it go. The Lord is saying, "I will be with you." He will help you overcome whatever you are going through. The Lord told Joshua to act according to the law that Moses had given him, not to turn to the right or the left. Most of the time when God wants us to do something, he gives us instructions. When we mess up his instructions, it takes time before the work can be accomplished, but because he is a merciful God and a God of second chances, he always allows us more time to get back and follow his instructions. The Lord told Joshua, "When you follow my instructions, you will be successful wherever you go." Sometimes we miss our success because we do not want to follow or do not understand God's directions. He also told Joshua that the book of the law should not depart from his mouth but to meditate upon it day and night. He told him again to be strong and courageous, not to be frightened or dismayed, "for the Lord your God will be with you wherever you go."

Sometimes we get to the point of being frightened. I do not know if you have gotten to that point of being frightened, but I myself have multiple times. I have been dismayed, but the Lord told Joshua, "I will be with you wherever you go." I was frightened when I was waiting for my NCLEX results because I thought I had failed, but God gave me the courage and strength to wait. God is going to be with you wherever you go. Are you frightened or dismayed? Hold on to God and his Word, and he will be with you in your exam room.

As students, we need to follow our instructors' instructions. I have found myself getting low grades on my papers because of not following directions. Sometimes it is not that I refused to follow directions, but that I misunderstood and did something different from what my instructor wanted. I just finished doing a speech class online. I had to submit a video, and the instructor wanted me to submit the works cited and the outline as a Word document. Instead of submitting a Word document, I submitted a URL, and she deducted some points. Following directions is very important. Sometimes we misunderstand God and do things differently, but God gives us another chance to correct ourselves. To succeed, make sure you follow your instructors' instructions. Instructors have been where you are and understand it better than students.

Matthew 28:18–20 talks about the authority that Jesus gave the disciples and how he told them he would be with them. Jesus tells them that as they go and make disciples of others, he will be with them until the end of the ages. In our studies, God is going to be with us. In our daily work God is going to be with us. We have power and authority to overcome each and every obstacle, challenge, and frustration that comes on our way. So this is not only an Old

Testament promise but a New Testament promise that God will be with us. Are you planning to give up? Please do not, because I have good news: God is going to be with you and will help you overcome what is ahead of you. Everything that has a name has to bow, and everything in life has an expiration date. The expiration date of your problem is coming, and very soon it will be history.

Maybe you are reading this book but do not know Jesus as your Lord and Savior. I want to let you know that the greatest gift you can have is accepting Jesus into your life. Everything will pass away, but the name of the Lord will remain forever. When Jesus healed the man at the pool of Bethesda, he told him to sin no more or something worse would happen to him. "Later Jesus found him at the temple and said to him, 'See, you are well again. Stop sinning or something worse may happen to you.' The man went away and told the Jewish leaders that it was Jesus who had made him well" (John 5:14–15).

Jesus gave him a miracle of physical healing, but the most important miracle Jesus gave him was spiritual healing—forgiveness of his sin. Jesus can give you education, and physical and emotional healing, but the most important gift of all is forgiveness of your sin. Pray this prayer with me: "Jesus, I come to you. I know you love me. I pray that you forgive my sins and accept me into your kingdom. Cleanse me with your blood. I know I cannot make it in life without you. Deliver me from every evil and temptation from the enemy. In Jesus' name I pray, amen." Look for a church that can help you grow in Christ. Confess to someone about the salvation of Jesus Christ. Start reading the Word of God to help you grow spiritually.

Printed in the United States
By Bookmasters